Getting StartED with Windows Live Movie Maker

James Floyd Kelly

friendsof ⊖ ™

an Apress® company

GETTING STARTED with Windows Live Movie Maker

Copyright © 2010 by James Floyd Kelly

ISBN-13 (pbk): 978-1-4302-2901-8

ISBN-13 (electronic): 978-1-4302-2902-5

Printed and bound in the United States of America 9 8 7 6 5 4 3 2 1

Trademarked names may appear in this book. Rather than use a trademark symbol with every occurrence of a trademarked name, we use the names only in an editorial fashion and to the benefit of the trademark owner, with no intention of infringement of the trademark.

Distributed to the book trade worldwide by Springer-Verlag New York, Inc., 233 Spring Street, 6th Floor, New York, NY 10013. Phone 1-800-SPRINGER, fax 201-348-4505, e-mail orders-ny@springer-sbm.com, or visit www.springeronline.com.

For information on translations, please e-mail rights@apress.com or visit www.apress.com.

Apress and friends of ED books may be purchased in bulk for academic, corporate, or promotional use. eBook versions and licenses are also available for most titles. For more information, reference our Special Bulk Sales–eBook Licensing web page at www.apress.com/info/bulksales.

The source code for this book is freely available to readers at www.friendsofed.com in the Downloads section.

Credits

President and Publisher:
Paul Manning

Coordinating Editor:
Kelly Moritz

Lead Editor:
Ben Renow-Clarke

Copy Editor:
Tracy Brown Collins

Technical Reviewer:
Christopher Smith

Compositors:
MacPS, LLC

Editorial Board:
Clay Andres, Steve Anglin, Mark Beckner, Ewan Buckingham, Gary Cornell, Jonathan Gennick, Jonathan Hassell, Michelle Lowman, Matthew Moodie, Duncan Parkes, Jeffrey Pepper, Frank Pohlmann, Douglas Pundick, Ben Renow-Clarke, Dominic Shakeshaft, Matt Wade, Tom Welsh

Indexers:
BIM Indexing

Artist:
April Milne

Cover Designer:
Anna Ishchenko

For Jeff – Jedi Redneck and Video Master

Contents at a Glance

Contents

About the Author

James Floyd Kelly is a freelance writer living in Atlanta, Georgia, with degrees in English and Industrial Engineering. He has written books on a variety of subjects including netbooks, free software, building your own computer, and LEGO robotics. He is editor-in-chief of the world's most popular LEGO NXT robotics blog, thenxtstep.com, which continues to draw an estimated 50,000+ readers monthly, and is a regular contributor to the LEGO Mindstorm development team. His most recent book, *Build Your Own CNC Machine*, is the first book to include step-by-step instructions for building your very own computer controlled cutting and milling machine. When not writing, he and his wife enjoy time with their 3 year old son and are anxiously awaiting on the arrival of his new baby brother.

About the Technical Reviewer

Christopher R. Smith explores every interest that snags a moment in ponder. A decade as Senior Quality Assurance Inspector in the Shuttle Avionics Integration Laboratory at NASA's Johnson Space Center in Houston, Texas furnished opportunities where his innovations were recognized by NASA with a prestigious Space Act Award. Toiling over LEGO elements, CAD'ing building instructions, being part of the MINDSTORMS community as an MDP and MCP for LEGO, as well as, having fun with his fellow bloggers of The NXT Step provides the creative exploration he enjoys the most. Chris believes that everything is possible and our world is what we make of it.

Acknowledgments

The Friends of ED and Apress crews really do make writing a book enjoyable. From the proposal stage all the way to signing off on the text and cover, these teams really helped to make my writing life a little easier. This was a fun book to write, and I really do hope to work on many more projects with this group of folks. All of their names are listed a few pages back, but I'd like to single out Ben Renow-Clarke, Dominic Shakeshaft, Fran Parnell, Kelly Moritz, Tracy Brown Collins and Jonathan Gennick and give them a big *Thank You – Thumbs Up – Job Well Done* congratulations.

Chris Smith is a good friend who volunteered to work as the technical editor and, rather than believe me when I told him the chapters were perfect, dug deep and proved me wrong by finding some errors that I've since corrected.

Finally, a big hug and thanks to my wife, Ashley, for enduring life as the spouse of a writer. She puts up with my odd writing times and my stress and moods when due dates are looming.

Introduction

If you've ever watched a friend or family member's home movies and wished you were home doing the laundry because it would be much more exciting, then you might find this book useful.

If you've ever watched your friends and family members try to stay awake, fidget, and watch the ceiling fan spin while watching one of your home movies, then you might find this book useful, too.

Either way, there is always room for improvement when it comes to homemade movies. While you have no control over other people's movies, you do have control over your own. There are plenty of computer applications out there that will allow you to edit your movies, add music, pull in special effects, and tweak opening and closing credits. But not all of them are easy to use or easy to afford. The easy applications always seem to come with a high price... and the complicated ones seem to come with an even higher price!

Well, not anymore.

While Microsoft continues to charge for its newest and most popular operating system, Windows 7, and its productivity suite, Office, it does occasionally give away some really nice software. And one of those freebies just happens to be a great little video editing application called Windows Live Movie Maker, or Movie Maker for short.

Windows Live Movie Maker could very well be the only video editing software that 90% of the world needs. It doesn't come with a lot of technical support. But it is 100% free. And it doesn't come with a big manual. But it's 100% free. And it only runs on Windows Vista or Windows 7. But it's 100% free.

And best of all — it's extremely easy to use. I know that you've heard that before, but believe me — I'm not a video editing guru. Movie Maker has allowed me to take my home movies and make them much more enjoyable to watch, more eye-catching to my viewers, and a lot easier to share with the world. And I've documented all my experiences here, in a single manual to prove how easy this application is to download, install, and use.

It's so easy, in fact, that after uploading your videos from camera to hard drive, you can have your first movie created, complete with opening and closing credits, in less than five minutes. I'm not kidding.

Movie Maker is all you need to get started (well, that and a video camera and computer running Vista or Windows 7). Welcome to the world of digital video editing and movie creation with Movie Maker- it's fun, it's easy, and it's addictive.

Chapter 1

Windows Live Movie Maker

I take photos and videos of everything. Yes, I'm one of those people. I document just about everything I do. And I don't limit myself to the standard "special occasions" such as vacations, first steps, and weddings. No, I take pictures of things I build, such as a set of workbenches I recently cut and bolted together; I capture screenshots of software settings I've figured out; and I shoot video of me assembling things such as a 300+ piece LEGO robotics kit. The list goes on.

But I don't stop at taking photos and videos. No sir. I collect all my photos, images, and videos on my laptop and then make a backup of everything on both a DVD and an external hard drive. (Yes, I'm a little neurotic about backing up my stuff.) But that's still not where it ends.

I'm also one of those people that likes to share this stuff. No, I don't force it on anyone who isn't interested — I'm not in the habit of cornering my friends and neighbors in front of the TV to watch videos of the previous summer's vacation. And I certainly don't bury my visitors in stacks of photo albums dating from 1992 to yesterday.

Instead, I like to collect my photos and videos and apply a little creative licensing and editing to them. I prefer to do a little culling and a little cropping and make these digital files much more fun to share with friends and family. Because, let's face it: just because I shot two hours of my wife touring some Mayan ruins, doesn't mean that my in-laws want to spend two hours on the couch watching her walk around, sneeze, sigh, and wait in line. No, they want to see the good stuff. The best pictures and snippets of video I can provide. The highlights.

So that's what I give them. My videos are carefully edited, and my pictures are nicely cropped. I add some background music here and some voiceover there; I throw some nice transitions between scenes into the mix, and everything is saved so it can be shared using my audience's desired method of delivery: email, pen drive, YouTube, or even a DVD.

Yes, I care about my audience. I want them to enjoy my photos and videos, not be bored by them. And that's why I use Windows Live Movie Maker (Movie Maker for short), an application from Microsoft that will allow you to entertain your friends and family, too. Movie Maker enables you to take control of your videos and photos and create fun and engaging digital video presentations to share with the world. It's easy to get, easy to learn, and easy to use. And it's free.

So, what are you waiting for? Are you ready to start putting together your own award-winning videos (okay, that's a stretch, but your friends and family would probably give you awards if they could)? Are you ready to see just how quick and easy it is to take those boring videos and pictures and give them some flash and pop? Are you curious to know how easy it is to share your final creation with others? If so, then you've got the right book.

In this chapter, I'm first going to show you where to download Movie Maker and how to install it. Next, I'll give you a quick overview of the application, including its new look and some of its features. After that, the rest of the book is going to explain how to best use Movie Maker and its special features to make your photo and videos come alive. Let's have some fun!

Downloading Movie Maker

Getting a free copy of Movie Maker is simple. Point your web browser to download.live.com and you'll see the screen shown in Figure 1-1.

Welcome to Windows Live Essentials. Windows Live Essentials will give you access to a variety of free applications and services, not just Movie Maker. But in order to get that access, you'll need a Windows Live ID. If you already have one, click the Sign In button in the upper right-hand corner of the screen and enter your Live ID and password to login. If you don't have a Live ID, click the Sign Up button that appears and follow the instructions to get your Live ID and password. (You can change the password supplied by Microsoft Live later if you like.)

Once you've signed in, you'll be returned to the screen shown in Figure 1-1. Windows Live Essentials consists of seven different applications: Messenger, Mail, Writer, Photo Gallery, Movie Maker, Family Safety, and Toolbar. You'll be given the option to select any or all of these applications to install after downloading a single installer application.

Figure 1-1. A Windows Live account is required for downloading Movie Maker.

Now that you're logged in, click the *Download* button seen in Figure 1-1 and you'll be taken to a new screen, shown in Figure 1-2.

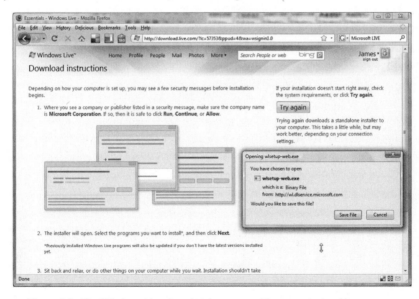

Figure 1-2. The Windows Live download page provides more instructions.

A pop-up window will appear that will allow you to save the installation file (called wlsetup-web.exe) to your hard drive. Click the *Save File* button and the file will be downloaded to your computer. (The default location is different for different web browsers, but will most likely be in the Download folder or on your desktop.)

Once the file has finished downloading, it's time to install Movie Maker.

Installing Movie Maker

Double-click the wlsetup-web.exe file that you downloaded in the previous section. You'll see a screen like the one in Figure 1-3.

Figure 1-3. The Windows Live Installer will begin the installation process.

After the Installer has been loaded, a new screen will display as shown in Figure 1-4.

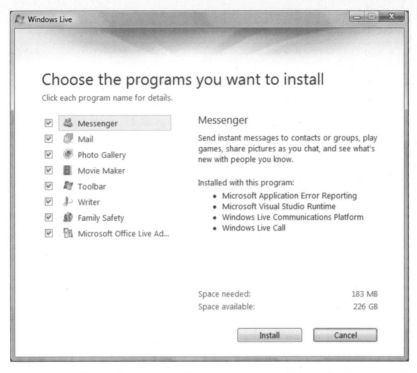

Figure 1-4. The Windows Live Installer lets you choose which applications to install.

Click an application once to read a description of the program on the right side of the screen. Feel free to install any of the applications you like, but make certain that the little box to the left of Movie Maker has a checkmark. Click the box to the left of any application you do not want installed to remove the checkmark. You can also see how much hard drive space is needed and available on this screen. When you are ready, click the *Install* button.

Figure 1-5 shows how the Windows Live Installer will provide you an update on the installation as a percentage.

Figure 1-5. Your Windows Live applications begin to install.

When completed, you'll see a screen like the one in Figure 1-6. You can check or uncheck the boxes, depending on whether you'd like to perform these final actions. I chose to uncheck all the boxes. I don't need to change my homepage or set my Internet search provider, and providing digital feedback to Microsoft about my computer's settings isn't something I feel comfortable doing. But feel free to leave that box checked if you like.

Figure 1-6. Your Windows Live applications are installed and ready to use.

Click the *Continue* button shown in Figure 1-6. Once again, you'll be asked to sign in with your Live ID, as shown in Figure 1-7. Click the *Close* button.

Now all that's left is to open the Movie Maker application to verify that it installed successfully. Click *Start* ➤ *All Programs* ➤ *Windows Live* ➤ *Windows Live Movie Maker* to open the application.

If Movie Maker installed properly, you should be greeted by a screen like the one shown in Figure 1-8.

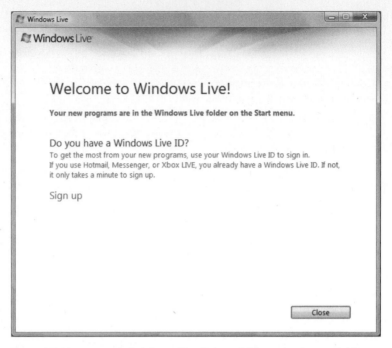

Figure 1-7. You are reminded that a Live ID is useful for accessing special features.

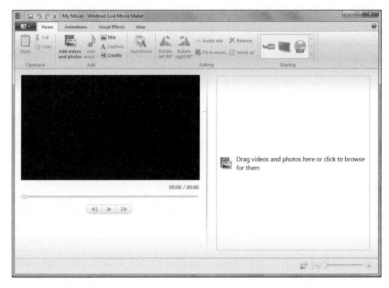

Figure 1-8. Movie Maker – ready for you to start making great movies.

Introducing Movie Maker

Windows Live Movie Maker (or Movie Maker for short) is, at its simplest, an application for creating a digital video that can be saved and played back in various formats including a DVD or a digital movie file stored on your hard drive or uploaded to the very popular online video site, YouTube. It helps you organize and edit your photos and videos (whether from a digital video recorder or even a mobile phone) and create a larger, more polished, and professional looking video. Movie Maker allows you to crop photos, edit videos, and add music and narration: all the things that make a great video, well … great!

Here's a short list of some of the things that users have done with Movie Maker:

- Vacation DVD: Movie Maker is perfect for taking your vacation photos and videos and organizing them into a more useful structure on a DVD. Think about the menu system found on a movie DVD: Main Movie, Bloopers, Photo Gallery, Interviews, and so on. Well, you can do the same thing with your vacation files and create a DVD that allows the viewer to select only those things they want to view and nothing else.

- Instructional video: Movie Maker allows you to edit your videos and then apply transitions, such as fading in or fading out, to give the video a more polished look. With the ability to record a narration over the edited video, companies and individuals can create instructional videos quickly and easily. Imagine how your customers would respond to a DVD containing video instructions instead of a typical black-and-white printed instruction manual!

- Photo montage: Not every movie has to have actual video. Some of the best videos are simply a collection of photos that fade in and out or blend together, creating an eye-catching and entertaining slideshow. Add in some subtle background music (you can control the volume with Movie Maker), and you've got something much more engaging than a photo album, with larger images displayed on your computer screen or television.

- Family reunion: Imagine being able to provide each and every family member with a DVD that contains a mixture of video and photos from a family reunion. Movie Maker allows you to create DVDs directly from within the application, including designing a menu system for navigating and selecting from videos, photos, and even a video with scrolling text that provides Aunt Mabel's secret family recipe for potato soup.

- School presentation: These days, anyone can put together a presentation using a slideshow application such as Microsoft PowerPoint, but many students have found these applications lacking when it comes to adding video and special effects such as music and transitions. Movie Maker can give students much more flexibility and allow them to stretch their creativity even further than the old fashioned slideshow.

Given all that it can do (the previous list and much more), Movie Maker is a little application and can be a bit misleading the first time you open it. Movie Maker's simple user interface is shown in Figure 1-9 and, as you can see, there's not a lot to see at first. But hidden in this great application is a nice sized collection of special features that can add powerful effects to your final project.

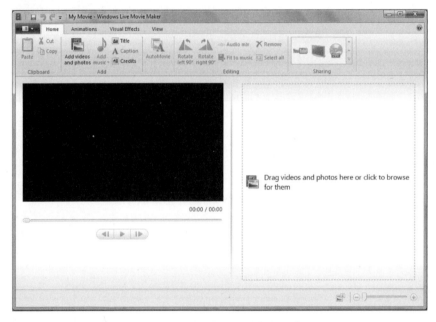

Figure 1-9. Windows Live Movie Maker has a simple interface.

Movie Maker's user interface is broken into five sections: the *File* menu, the Ribbon, the Library, a Currently Editing section, and a Library Control toolbar. You will use each of these sections to perform special actions to your videos and photos.

ExplainED

With Movie Maker, you can add image files that aren't necessarily photos taken with a digital camera. Movie Maker supports a variety of file types including .jpg, .tif, and .png. Throughout the book, whenever I use the word "photo," please remember that this can include other graphical files such as screen captures and scanned documents and drawings from applications such as Paint, among others.

The File Menu

Figure 1-10 shows the *File* menu expanded. As with most applications, the *File* menu provides functions that apply to the entire document. Access the *File* menu by clicking the small downward-pointing arrow shown in Figure 1-10.

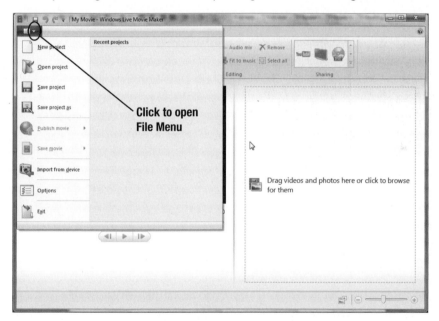

Figure 1-10. The Movie Maker File menu lets you save, rename, and more.

I'll be covering all of the various options available to you from the *File* menu in later chapters. For now, however, just know that the *File* menu is where you'll be saving your work, creating new projects, and opening existing projects.

Other options that we'll examine later include importing files from digital devices and publishing your finished movies.

The Ribbon

The Ribbon is new to many Microsoft products. It's a new interface design that attempts to group application functions and make them visible only when you need them. Take a look at Figure 1-11, for example. The Ribbon runs along the top of the Movie Maker application and consists of a variety of tabs, including *Home, Animations, Visual Effects,* and *View.*

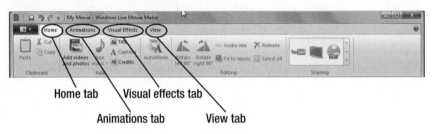

Figure 1-11. The Movie Maker Ribbon groups features using tabs.

NotED

More tabs can appear on the Ribbon depending on what you are doing within Movie Maker. For example, when working with videos, an Edit tab will appear (like the one seen in Figure 1-12) that provides certain editing tools (such as fade ins) specific to videos. The same Edit tab will appear when working with photos, but the options available will be slightly different since you're working with a photo, not a video.

In Figure 1-11, I have the *Home* tab selected. Look closely and you'll see options such as *Add Video and Photos, Title, Credits,* and *Rotate Right 90 degrees.* Don't worry about what these do right now; instead, click the *Animations* tab. You'll notice that the *Home* tab options disappear and are replaced with the ones shown in Figure 1-12.

Figure 1-12. The Movie Maker Animations tab has some interesting buttons.

The *Animation* tab contains exactly what the name implies: choices of animation that can be applied to your videos or photos. These include slides, flips, and pixelations. Don't worry if you're not familiar with those terms; you'll learn all about them in Chapters 5 and 6.

Figure 1-13 shows the *Visual Effects* tab. As with the Animation tab, this tab's features are all about making your videos and photos more eye-catching.

Figure 1-13. The Movie Maker Visual Effects tab has even more fun features to offer.

Finally, Figure 1-14 shows the *View* tab.

Figure 1-14. The View tab lets you customize the way files are displayed on screen.

The options available on the *View* tab allow you to change the size of the photos and videos that you are working on in the Library. What's the Library? Glad you asked.

The Library

When you select videos and photos to include in your movie project, those files will appear in the right-hand panel of the screen indicated in Figure 1-15. This panel is called the Library.

ExplainED

How do you differentiate between a photo and a video in the Library? Take a close look in Figure 1-15 and you should be able to see a set of dashed squares running down the left or right side of some of the images. These dashed squares are supposed represent "video film," which is slightly humorous in that most video these days is shot using digital devices that store video on digital memory and not celluloid film. The "film" marks appear on the left side of an image to indicate the start of the video, and the marks will appear on the right side of an image to indicate the end of the video. Photos and images are simply bounded on the left and right by black bars.

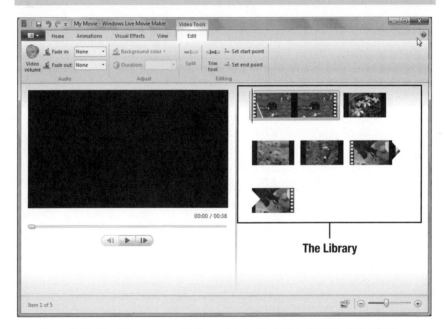

Figure 1-15. The Library can contain a mixture of photos, images, and videos.

In a nutshell, icons in the Library represent individual videos or pictures that you've imported. Pictures will run for a default of five seconds (this can be changed, however), but videos will run for their full recording length. The Library is easy to use: simply click an icon to select it. If it's a video, you can use the Play/Pause controls in the Current Editing Section on the left side of the screen (covered next) to watch that particular video. If it's a photo, it will simply be displayed in the Current Editing box on the left side of the screen.

I'll cover using the Library more in later chapters, but before I move on, I'd like to explain that any videos or photos in the Library can be individually selected by clicking one of them. When you click a video or photo, you indicate to Movie Maker that you wish to perform some actions to that item. Movie Maker, in turn, takes the photo or video you clicked and places it in the Current Editing Section, covered next.

The Current Editing Section

Just like it sounds, the Current Editing Section is where you'll be doing most of your work. A video or photo clicked in the Library will appear in this pane, and you'll have access to all the tools and features found on the Ribbon that can make changes to that video or photo. Figure 1-16 shows the Current Editing Section with a video selected from the Library.

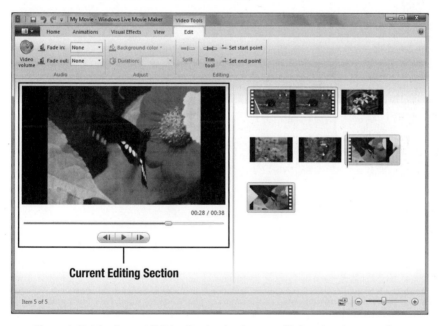

Figure 1-16. The Current Editing Section is where you'll do most of your work.

Remember, you'll be selecting videos and photos from the Library and editing and adding effects to them from within the Current Editing Section. This means you can only edit a single video or a single image at any given time. You'll gain a better understanding of this in Chapter 2, where I show you how to do a few simple edits to a video and photo.

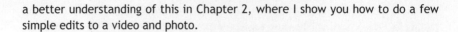

Take a closer look at Figure 1-16, and you'll notice a thin black line running along the left edge of one of the videos. The black line is a visual indicator to help you quickly determine which video or photo is selected for editing in the Current Editing Section.

The Library Control Toolbar

The last section of Movie Maker that I'd like to cover is the Library Control Toolbar, shown in Figure 1-17.

Library Control Bar

Figure 1-17. The Library Control Toolbar is small and easy to overlook.

The Library Control Toolbar doesn't have a lot of features, but it is useful when trying to figure out which item (video or photo) you are working on or when you wish to enlarge or shrink the size of the items displayed in the Library.

In the lower-left corner, you'll always find a total count of the number of items in the Library. In Figure 1-17, this count is 5, and the toolbar also tells me that I'm currently editing item 4 of 5. But this item count can change. Over in the lower right-hand corner, you'll see a drag bar that can expand or decrease the number of icons in the Library. I've dragged the bar to the right to increase the icons, and you can see the results in Figure 1-18.

Figure 1-18. Use the drag bar to increase or decrease the number of Library icons.

Why would I want to change the number of the icons? I'll cover this in more detail in later chapters, but for now what you need to understand is that videos and photos will both have a specific length of time that they will display in your final movie. A 45-second video of a bear, for example, can be displayed as two icons, as seen in Figure 1-17, or as three icons, as seen in Figure 1-18. By breaking up a video into parts, you can jump forward (in time) or backward to find that specific part of a video that you are interested in adding to your video. This may not be so apparent with a short, 20-second video, but when you have 40 minutes of your cousin's three year old opening gifts, you'll appreciate the ability to jump to the best parts and then crop the video to show only those two or three minutes. The drag bar allows you to expand your videos by breaking them into more manageable (and more easily viewed) parts.

ExplainED

Expanding the view to increase the number of Library icons does not modify the video in any way; it simply allows you to zoom in or out on a particular video and begin playing it (for editing purposes) from any point in the video. Normally when you click a single video icon in the Library, the video will be reset to play from the beginning. By dividing the video into more icons (for example, three for a 45-second video) you could select the second video and begin watching and editing that video from the 15-second mark rather than starting over at the beginning.

With increasing or decreasing the number of icons in the Library, however, it's worth pointing out that any special effects that you apply to a part of a video will be applied to the entire video, not just the individual part you happen to be editing. So, in Figure 1-18, if I apply a flip animation to the last 15 seconds of the bear video by selecting the third (of three) icons that represent that video, the flip animation will still be applied to the first 15 seconds and to the second 15 seconds.

NotED

There is a way around this, however. If you find that you'd like to apply a special effect to the first 30 seconds of a video and a completely different special effect to the last 30 seconds, the solution involves splitting a video. I'll cover this in more detail in Chapter 3.

Finally, if you click the *Change thumbnail size* icon on the Library Control Toolbar, you can change the visible size of the icons in the Library, as seen in Figure 1-19. Here, I've increased the Library icons so I can see more detail in the videos and photos. A scroll bar along the left edge will let me scroll down to view those icons that have been pushed off the screen.

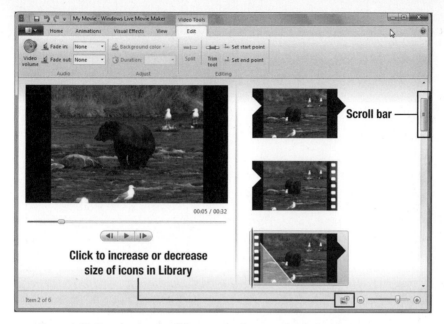

Figure 1-19. Use the thumbnail button to enlarge or shrink the Library icons.

That's it for the various sections of Movie Maker. You'll get a lot more practice in using them in upcoming chapters.

What's Next?

Now that you have an overview of Movie Maker and have the application installed, it's time to put it to work. In Chapter 2, I'm going to show you how fast and easy it is to create a movie, complete with title and credits, with the click of a single button. And while we're learning how to make a quick-and-easy movie, I'll also be introducing you to some other Movie Maker tools that enable you to import video and pictures, save your project, and try out a few special effects.

Chapter 2

Getting Started with AutoMovie

Movie Maker can help you put together some great videos to share with your friends and family. It has tons of special effects and powerful features to help clean up, edit, and add some "Pow!" to your final projects. But before you can begin creating great videos, you've got to have the *raw* pictures and video to work with.

What do I mean by raw? Raw video is the video that comes directly from your video camera: it includes all the mistakes, the jostles, bumps, and out-of-focus scenery that you really don't want included in your final movie. The same goes for photos; adding photos to your video is great, but you'll first want to crop, remove red-eye, and clean up other aspects of your photos, such as poor lighting and crookedness.

Using a variety of tricks and features I'll cover later in this book, raw photos and video can be turned into final photos and video that are cleaned up and ready to be added to your movie. But that isn't to say that you can't take raw video and photos and immediately make a movie to share; sometimes that's exactly what you want. Maybe you've shot three minutes of a speech or two minutes of a freefall skydive; in those instances, you may want to simply get the video ready for sharing with friends and family or the entire world with no editing whatsoever.

Well, this chapter is going to show you exactly how easy and fast it is to create a fast video using raw source material. It's called AutoMovie, and it's a built-in feature of Movie Maker. And to get you ready to use Movie Maker, I'm also going to start out by showing you how to gather and organize the raw video and photos from your digital equipment to make your video creation project go smoothly.

Importing Your Videos and Photos

Before I get started showing you how to create a video using AutoMovie, I need to cover the three methods for obtaining the videos and photos that you'll be using in your projects. There are three methods:

1. Download via your Digital Device's Special Software.
2. Download via a Memory Stick or CD/DVD.
3. Direct Download from within Movie Maker.

Let me briefly explain how each method works. You'll want to decide which methods work best for you based on the digital camera and digital recorder that you are using. You may find yourself using one method for a digital camera and another method for a digital recorder. That's perfectly acceptable; the goal is to get your digital photo and video files transferred to your computer's hard drive so you can start using Movie Maker.

ExplainED

Throughout this book, I'm going to use the term "digital device" to describe both digital cameras and digital recorders. For most devices, you'll find very similar methods for copying or moving files from the device to your hard drive. When in doubt, consult the digital device's user manual for specific instructions.

Downloading Via a Digital Device's Special Software

When you purchase a digital camera or recorder, you'll more than likely find a CD or DVD in the box that contains not only the device's driver (the special files needed for your operating system to "talk" to the device), but also some sort of special software for downloading files from the device to your computer.

Using your device's special software is typically considered the safest and most reliable method for pulling your files from the device to your computer, and I highly recommend testing this software so you'll become comfortable with how it is used.

Sometimes this software will automatically open when it detects that you've connected the device to your computer using a cable, such as a USB cable. And sometimes you'll have to open the software on your own and let it detect the connected device.

Figure 2-1 shows a special application that opens automatically when I connect my Sony digital camera. I have the option of clicking the Cancel button to shut it down; this is a nice option, because I prefer to let Movie Maker import my digital photos. (This is the third option I'll be discussing shortly.)

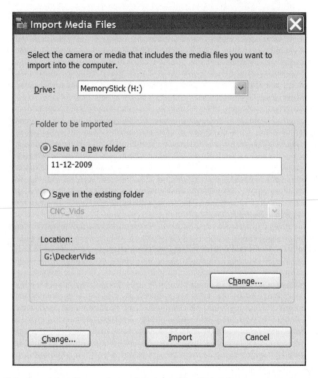

Figure 2-1. Special software is used to transfer photos from camera to computer.

If I choose to let the special software access my digital camera, it will allow me to view all the photos stored on the camera's memory card and select those I wish to transfer to my hard drive. Notice also in Figure 2-1 that I can select the location where I wish to save the files by using the Change button. Your software likely offers the same options, so be sure to read the Help files or instructions so you'll always be able to save your files where you can easily access them.

The same process exists for digital recorders. Most recorders come with special software that you'll use to transfer your raw video from the device to your computer. (Once again, some digital recorders are able to have their video transferred directly to the hard drive via Movie Maker.)

Using your digital devices' special software is a safe and reliable method for moving your files from device to computer. Give it a try if you've not yet used it and see if you like the process.

Downloading Via a Memory Stick or CD/DVD

The second method I'd like to introduce to you involves removing a storage medium from your digital camera or digital recorder. Figure 2-2 shows a memory stick that I've removed from my Sony digital camera. My Sony digital recorder uses mini-CDs, as shown in Figure 2-3.

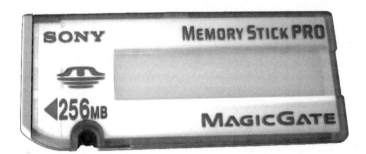

Figure 2-2. Memory cards are used most often with digital cameras.

In both instances, my digital devices have a storage medium that, given the right hardware in my computer, I can remove and insert into my computer to transfer the files.

Memory cards comes in a variety of formats, so you'll want to make sure that your computer (or laptop) has a memory card reader that supports the card found in your camera.

Figure 2-3. Many video recorders use mini-CD or mini-DVD technology.

NotED

Believe it or not, many digital video recorders also record video to memory cards. Memory cards are getting cheaper at the same time that they are increasing their storage size. If you're in the market for a digital video recorder, you may want to give serious consideration to purchasing one that records to memory cards instead of discs (CD or DVD).

To transfer files from a memory card, you simply insert the card into the memory card reader. The memory card is typically treated just like an external hard drive or pen drive. It shows up with its own drive letter (see Figure 2-4), and files can be copied, moved, and deleted to and from the memory card as with any standard device.

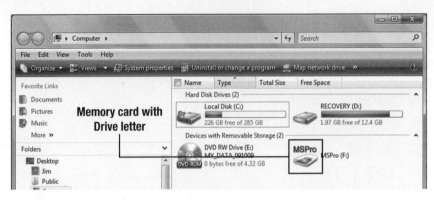

Figure 2-4. Memory cards are treated as external storage devices.

LinkED

If your laptop or computer doesn't have a memory card reader, you'll be happy to hear that you can purchase an inexpensive card reader that connects to your computer via a USB port. Some of the more popular USB memory card readers come from Kingston. You can find more details on these devices by visiting www.kingston.com/flash/readers.asp.

Using Mini-CDs or Mini-DVDs does require a CD or DVD drive in your computer. But before you remove the CD or DVD from your digital recorder, there is one step you must typically perform. It's sometimes called finalizing or closing, and what it means is simply that the digital recorder must prepare the CD or DVD so it can be read by a CD/DVD drive in your computer. Every digital recorder does this differently, so be sure to consult your user manual for the steps required to prepare a mini-CD or mini-DVD for use in your computer or laptop's CD/DVD drive.

Once you insert the CD/DVD in the drive however, it works just like a normal CD or DVD; browse to the folder that contains the video you wish to transfer to your computer's hard drive and copy it over. (You most likely will not be able to move or delete the original from the CD/DVD if it has been prepared as described earlier.)

Whether you transfer files to your hard drive by inserting a memory card into a memory card reader or by reading these files from a mini-CD/DVD, having the raw files located on your hard drive puts you one step closer to putting together a great video project.

Direct Download from Within Movie Maker

The third method for getting videos and photos to your hard drive for use with Movie Maker is just as quick and easy as the previous two methods. It involves opening Movie Maker, clicking the File menu, and selecting *Import From Device,* as seen in Figure 2-5.

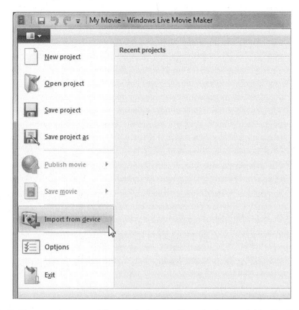

Figure 2-5. You can import video and photos directly from within Movie Maker.

When the screen shown in Figure 2-6 appears, Movie Maker is waiting for you to connect your digital camera or recorder to the computer with a USB cable. After connecting the device, it should appear on the screen; if it does not appear, click the *Refresh* button.

ExplainED

If your device does not appear on the list, then it is likely your device is an older one, and Movie Maker will not recognize it from within the application. In this situation, you will have to use one of the other two methods for getting files to your hard drive. Transfer files using either your device's special software or by reading its storage medium (card or CD/DVD).

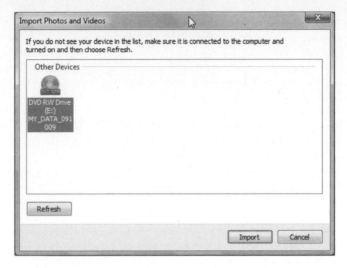

Figure 2-6. Movie Maker waits for you to connect your digital camera or recorder.

Figure 2-7 shows the icon that appears after I plug in my digital camera. Notice that it is given a drive letter (F:) and labeled as a Removable Disk.

Figure 2-7. Movie Maker can import directly from a digital device.

Click the new icon once and then click the *Import* button. You will see a screen like the one shown in Figure 2-8. You're given the total number of pictures (or videos) found on the device, as well as the option to select which files you want to pull off the device. (You can also select to download everything immediately without review.) Make your selection and click the *Next* button.

NotED

When transferring movies or photos from a digital device, try to always have the digital device plugged in using its own power supply. If the batteries were to die in your device during file transfer, there is a risk that you might lose one or more files while they are being transferred.

Figure 2-8. Import all files or choose to select only those files you want.

If you choose the first option, shown in Figure 2-8, (*Review, Organize, and Group Items to Import*), you'll see a screen like the one in Figure 2-9. From here, you can select (or deselect by removing the checkbox next to a group of photos) the photos you wish to import. Click the *Import* button when you're ready to start the import process.

ExplainED

If you click the Expand All option in the lower left-hand corner of the window (Figure 2-9), each group that is selected (with a check in the checkbox) will expand, allowing you to see each photo in that group. Then, you can remove the checkmark next to the individual photos within a group that you choose not to import.

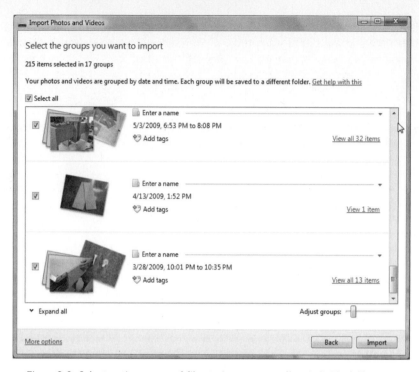

Figure 2-9. Select entire groups of files to import, as well as individual files.

Photos are then imported into the Pictures folder (or My Pictures) and stored in a folder with the current date as its title (see Figure 2-10). Browse to those photos and then copy (or move) the ones you wish to use with Movie Maker into a storage folder labeled "Raw photos" or something like that. (In the next section, I'll explain how to create a folder structure that will make editing and saving your files much easier.)

Figure 2-10. Photos are stored in the Pictures folder.

Before we move on to creating a video using AutoMovie, I want to show you the importing process with a video recorder instead of a camera. After plugging in my digital video camera with the USB cable, I click the new icon shown in Figure 2-11 and click the *Import* button. Notice the icon is labeled *DVD RW Drive (F:)*. For all practical purposes, my digital recorder shows up as a recordable DVD drive to Windows!

Figure 2-11. A digital camera's files can also be imported from within Movie Maker.

ExplainED

If the Movie Maker import feature does not list your digital recorder (even after clicking the Refresh button), then most likely your digital recorder is an older device that is not recognized by the latest version of Windows or Movie Maker. You'll need to import your videos using the special software that came with your digital recorder.

After clicking the import button, I once again have the choice of importing all the video files stored on the digital recorder, or I can pick and choose the videos I wish to transfer. Figure 2-12 shows that I've selected to pick the files I want before clicking the *Next* button.

31

Figure 2-12. Pick individual videos or choose to transfer all of them at once.

Next, I'm given the ability to select the videos I wish to transfer. Figure 2-13 shows how thumbnails are used to represent each video. It takes a little time for Movie Maker to examine each video, so in this figure you can see that only two of the X-number of videos have been scanned so far. After the video thumbnails are completed, I can uncheck a box to deselect a video or leave a video checked to indicate it will be downloaded from the digital recorder. I then click the *Import* button to start the transfer to my hard drive.

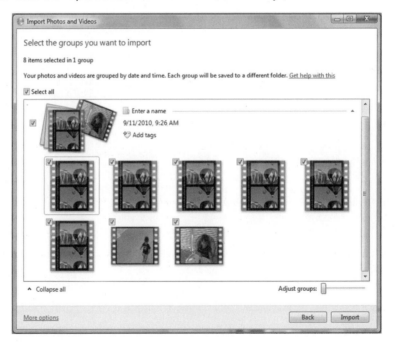

Figure 2-13. Select the videos you wish to transfer.

The import process can take some time, especially for lengthy videos. A screen like the one shown in Figure 2-14 will keep you informed on the transfer progress.

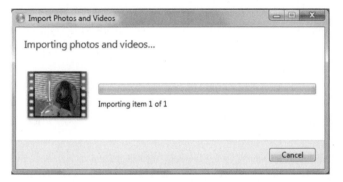

Figure 2-14. Importing videos can take some time.

When the import process is done, the videos will be stored in the Pictures (or My Pictures) folder, located in a folder with the current date as shown in Figure 2-15.

Figure 2-15. Your videos are now stored in the Pictures (or My Pictures) folder.

And that's it! Three different methods for transferring your photos and videos from device to hard drive. I encourage you to try all three methods using both your digital camera and your digital video recorder to determine which method is easiest for you. I prefer to use Movie Maker to import from the devices rather than removing my memory cards or mini-DVDs., but that's me. You may find that the special software that comes with your devices is even easier to use, or you may prefer to grab files directly from memory cards and CD/DVDs.

Whichever method you use, the goal is to get the files you will be working with in Movie Maker to your hard drive. But once the files are on your hard drive, there's still one more suggestion I'd like to make that will help you when it comes time to editing your photos and videos within Movie Maker.

Organizing Your Digital Files

Videos and pictures that you move to your computer's hard drive are often stored in different locations. Your pictures, for example, may be downloaded by default to the My Pictures folder. Likewise, your digital recorder's special software may download your video files to a special folder created just for that device's videos. Storing all the photos and videos in multiple locations will work, yes, but it's not the most efficient way to work with Movie Maker.

Rather than store videos and pictures in multiple locations, I feel that keeping these files stored together in a special project folder is the best way to keep track of your original files (the raw video and photos), your newly modified files, and the final video project.

Feel free to organize your files any way you like, but for most of the projects in this book that I'll be writing about, let me explain the following folder structure I'll be using and why:

Main Folder — Special Project Name

> Subfolder 1 – Raw photos

> Subfolder 2 – Raw videos

> Subfolder 3 – Working photos and videos

> Subfolder 4 – Final project

You can store the main folder and all its subfolders anywhere you like, but I recommend the My Documents folder (or the Documents folder in Windows Vista).

The Main Folder should be given a name that reflects the final video. Examples include "Ashley's Birthday 2009" or "First Skydive Jump." A descriptive name will allow you to differentiate one project from another.

Subfolder 1 and Subfolder 2 are where I store my original photos and my original videos, respectively. "Raw photos" is the name of the first subfolder, and it will hold all my photos. Subfolder 2 is titled "Raw videos" and, likewise, I'll be storing my raw video in this folder. Here's the important part: I will never edit, modify, or delete files from these subfolders. Anytime I wish to edit a video or crop a photo, for example, I will make a copy of that file and place it in Subfolder 3, the "Working photos and videos" folder.

When I wish to add a photo or video to the Movie Maker Library (see Chapter 1), I will browse to Subfolder 3 and only import files that are located in that folder. Why would I do this? If I should accidentally (or intentionally) modify a video or picture and wish to undo my work, I will always have the originals in Subfolders 1 and 2. As long as I don't import files from those two subfolders, I'll always have my original photos and videos and can start over. I simply copy a raw version of a file into Subfolder 3 and begin again.

As you work in Movie Maker, you'll be saving your project (before you convert it into an actual video) and the work you've performed. You need a folder to store your project, and that is the purpose of Subfolder 4, "Final project."

The Final Project folder can contain multiple files; this may happen if you decide to create different versions of a video, such as one with music and one without. The key point here is to create a subfolder where you can save the work you've done within Movie Maker and return to it at a later time.

Figure 2-16 shows this folder structure in action; the Main Folder is located in the My Documents folder on my laptop. The Main Folder is titled "Vacation in Mexico," and you can see that I've created the subfolders and labeled them as described earlier.

Figure 2-16. Keep videos and photos organized during the creation of your project.

Make it a habit to always work from a copy of a raw file, never the original. Using a folder structure like the one I've described will help you stay organized as you use Movie Maker to create your own videos. And when you're done with a project, you can burn the Main Folder and all its subfolders to a CD or DVD as a backup, and free up hard drive space for your next video project.

NotED

Another subfolder that I sometimes add to the list is titled Raw Audio. Later in the book I'll show you how to add background music and voiceovers to your videos, and having a subfolder to store your audio files will be useful. By creating a Raw Audio folder (for your original recordings) and a Working Audio folder (that contains a copy of the files in the Raw Audio folder), you'll never have to worry about accidentally deleting or editing your original files.

And now it's time for me to show you how easy it is to make a movie with your pictures and videos using AutoMovie. Once you understand how AutoMovie works and how well it puts together simple videos, you'll appreciate even more the additional features that Movie Maker offers for more advanced editing.

AutoMovie Magic

AutoMovie isn't going to win you any real awards, but what it will do is stitch together any photos and videos you've added to the Library, add a changeable title to your movie, and add a "By ..." credit line at the end. It will attempt a few simple special effects such as fades or transitions in between items and, if you've added some background music, AutoMovie will do its best to change the timing of how long the photos and videos are displayed so it matches up with the length of the song.

It doesn't sound like much, but the nice thing about AutoMovie is that it can add just the right amount of polish to a handful of photos and videos to give your final movie a completed look and feel.

But rather than telling you about AutoMovie, let me show you how easy it is to create a generated AutoMovie and apply a few changes to make it your own.

I'll start by filling the Library with some photos and videos. Rather than do some sort of random video, I've decided for this book to try and make some videos that will actually be useful, entertaining, and hopefully both. For this first video, I'm going to use AutoMovie to help me add some bells and whistles to a short video I made that demonstrates the wood and other supplies (wood screws) used to make a workbench for under $75.00.

ExplainED

This video will be part of a larger project that I will be creating throughout the book. In later chapters, I'll use this workbench project to not only demonstrate some of the special features that Movie Maker offers, but at the end of the book I'm going to pull all my work together by creating a DVD, complete with a menu that the viewer can use to select scenes and more.

So, what I've done in preparation for using the AutoMovie feature is to take some photos of the various components I purchased to build the workbench, as well as shoot a video of me describing all the components as I lay them out on the floor.

LinkED

You can download the raw files of many of my pictures and videos and follow along throughout the book. You can use these so you can get some practice using Movie Maker. To download the files, visit the book's page at www.friendsofed.com.

Figure 2-17 shows an example of one of the photos I took for my first AutoMovie. It's a picture of two sheets of plywood. Other photos were taken of 2x4s, screws, and other wood components.

Figure 2-17. A photo that will be included with my AutoMovie project.

Figure 2-18 shows my Library filling up with the various photos and the single video I shot. Remember, click the *Add videos and photos* button and browse to your folder(s) that contain the files you want to add.

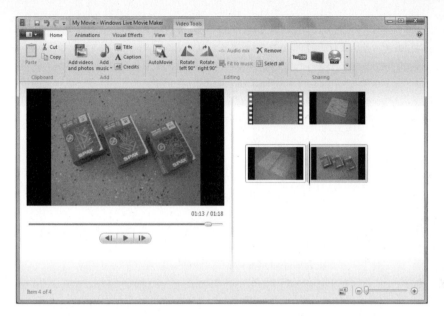

Figure 2-18. My AutoMovie will be made from a mix of photos and one video.

After importing all the photos and videos you wish to use to create your movie, you have one more option available before starting the AutoMovie process. You can drag photos and videos around in the Library to reorganize them. If you look at Figure 2-18, I've got the video first, followed by three photos. If I wish to have one or more photos displayed first in the movie, I simply click a photo and drag it to a new location. Figure 2-19 shows that I've placed all three photos in front of the video and I changed their order.

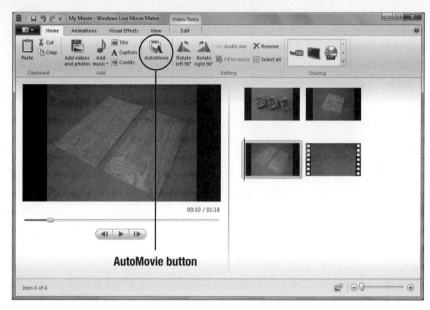

Figure 2-19. Reorganize videos and photos within the Library.

So, now it's time to create this movie. To do so, I simply click the *AutoMovie* button indicated in Figure 2-19. I then get an alert like the one shown in Figure 2-20.

Figure 2-20. Movie Maker will ask about adding music as a reminder.

For this first movie project, I'm not going to add any music or narration; I'm talking in the video, so I'll leave that alone for now by clicking *No*.

Making an AutoMovie doesn't take long. When the process is done, you'll see a message like the one in Figure 2-21. Click the *Close* button to continue and view your new movie.

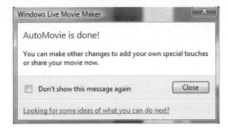

Figure 2-21. You will be alerted when the AutoMovie process is completed.

If you look closely at the Library, you'll notice some things have changed. As shown in Figure 2-22, I now have some text boxes added at the beginning and end of the Library window. One is *My Movie* and the other is *The End*.

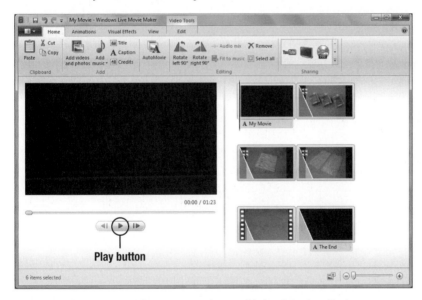

Figure 2-22. Your movie has some new items added to it by AutoMovie.

Notice also that some of the pictures have an angled line drawn from their upper left-hand corner to a point midway on the thumbnail icon. This icon is used to indicate some sort of special effect like a transition. More on that in a moment.

Go ahead and push the play button shown in Figure 2-22. Your movie will play, complete with opening title and closing credits. Did you also notice the subtle special effects added to the photos? The photos were given some slight animation by moving them around, as well as a fade-out and fade-in of the next photo. All this was done with the click of the AutoMovie button.

It's not much, I'll admit. Some text, some slight animation, followed by the movie and The End text. But this was done with no user input. Once you have an understanding of how easy it is to add your own text, special effects, and more, your movies will really come to life. AutoMovie is just the tip of the iceberg, so just keep in mind that we've only scratched the surface of Movie Maker features.

I'll be coming back to these photos and videos later in the book and showing you how to do more with them than what was demonstrated with AutoMovie. You can, for example, alter the title, change the closing credits, modify the background color, and even change the transitions between photos. And it's all fun and easy to do.

Now, before we say goodbye to the AutoMovie feature, there's one more item of business I need to show you. You don't want to lose all your hard work, so you're going to want to save your movie project so you can open it later and work on it some more, right?

Well, to do that, all that's required is for you to click the *File* menu and choose *Save Project* as shown in Figure 2-23.

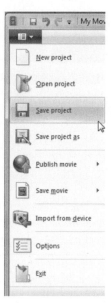

Figure 2-23. Be sure to save your project so you won't lose any of your work.

If you created your folder structure like I described earlier in this chapter, you'll want to give your project a name and save it in the "Final project" subfolder as shown in Figure 2-24.

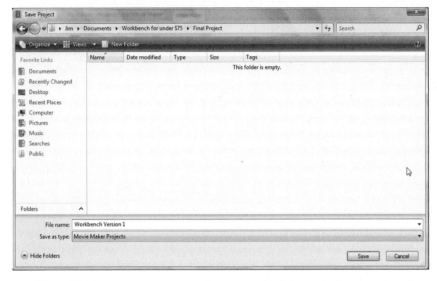

Figure 2-24. Be sure to save your project so you won't lose any of your work.

NotED

I've given this project the name of "Workbench Version 1," because I'm going to be doing some more work with it in later chapters and I'd like to be able to distinguish between each version. I recommend that you save each version of your movie as it develops under a different name; if a mistake should occur or you change your mind about the structure of your movie, you can always go back to a previous version and start over with your edits and special effects.

After saving your project, you can either continue working or close down Movie Maker until you wish to work on your project again. To open a project, simply open Movie Maker and choose *Open Project* from the *File* menu (see Figure 2-23) and browse to the location of your movie project file.

What's Next?

Now that you've seen how easy it is to import photos and videos into Movie Maker and make a movie using the AutoMovie feature, it's time to learn about the editing process. There are all kinds of things you can do to the photos and videos you will be adding to your movie, including flipping, rotating, cropping, and zooming in and out. I'll talk about widescreen versus normal (4:3) aspect and more about previewing your movies to see your changes (as well as reversing those changes if you don't like them). Chapter 3 is all about preparing your photos and videos for adding to your next movie. Let's see how that's done.

Chapter 3

Working with Video

There are a variety of tools available for editing photographs. It's fairly easy to remove redeye, fix a lighting issue, and tackle other problems that you encounter with your photos. Ideally, you want to clean up your photos before importing them into Movie Maker (applications such as PhotoShop, GIMP, and PaintShop Pro are all suitable solutions). But for videos, Movie Maker has some great editing tools built right in. You can simply import your videos into Movie Maker and then clean them up with some cropping, fade-ins, and more.

Before you can put together some great movies to share, however, you really need a solid understanding of how to properly edit within Movie Maker. In this chapter, I'm going to introduce you to all the editing features available and show you how to use them.

As you learn about editing your videos, keep in mind the old adage, "less is more." What do I mean by that? Have you ever watched a movie put together by a friend or family member that overwhelmed you with special effects? It is possible to over-edit your videos by cropping too frequently, including too many segments that are too short, or adding way too many transitions. I'll cover special effects in upcoming chapters, but for now, just keep in mind that the goal of editing is to provide the best stuff, the highlights, and keep your audience from growing bored. The flipside of this is that you can engage your audience with an interesting movie, but turn them off with poor editing and improper usage of sound, special effects, and video montages that jump from scene to scene too quickly.

I'll talk about this more throughout the book, but for now, let's jump in and take a look at Movie Maker's basic editing features and how they work. I encourage you to open Movie Maker and follow along with some of your own videos (or download some sample videos from the book's page at www.friendsofed.com).

Changing the Aspect Ratio

Video recorders capture video in numerous formats; .mpeg, .mov, and .avi are just a few of the typical movie formats that Movie Maker will accept.

NotED

For a complete list of all video and photo formats that Movie Maker supports, click the Help button in the upper right-hand corner of the Movie Maker application. The Windows Live Help Web site will open. Click the link in the left column labeled "What file types can I use in Windows Live Movie Maker?" and you can view a complete list of supported file types.

But no matter the format, it's likely that the video you shoot will only display in two aspects: 16:9 or 4:3. The aspect refers to the ratio of the width to height of the viewable area of the screen. Figure 3-1 shows a video that was taken using the standard 4:3 aspect that is typically used by non-widescreen televisions.

Figure 3-1. The 4:3 aspect ratio is found in most non-widescreen televisions.

You're already familiar with the 16:9 aspect ratio; it provides a wider image on the screen. Movie theaters typically project movies onto a 16:9 screen and most of today's video recorders also provide the ability to record in 16:9 aspect. This 16:9 aspect ratio is also often referred to as widescreen. Figure 3-2 shows the same video in Figure 3-1 displayed in widescreen format.

Figure 3-2. Widescreen or 16:9 format provides a wider viewing area.

Notice the black vertical bars along the left and right sides of the video? Those bars are added because the original video was shot in 4:3 format. Movie Maker is able to determine from most videos whether to display the video using a 4:3 or 16:9 aspect ratio. But not always. Video that is displayed using an incorrect aspect ratio will appear stretched or crushed; people and objects won't look right because they'll be stretched or compacted to fit the incorrect aspect ratio. To fix this problem, simply click the *Aspect ratio* button on the *View* tab indicated in Figure 3-3 and select the other aspect option.

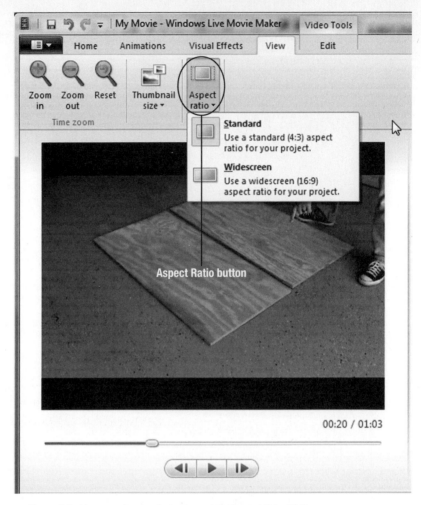

Figure 3-3. You can change the aspect ratio from 4:3 to 16:9.

Although this option is available to you, I recommend that you try and let Movie Maker make the best selection for the aspect ratio. Changing the aspect often simply shrinks the video to fit in the editing screen. To demonstrate this, I've imported a video shot in widescreen. This video can be seen in Figure 3-4.

Figure 3-4. A widescreen video uses the maximum display area.

After I select the Standard (4:3) aspect ratio, you can see in Figure 3-5 that all Movie Maker has done is shrink and fit the video so it fits in the 4:3 aspect ratio display; it will add horizontal bars along the top and bottom of the video to force the video fit the 4:3 screen size. The black bars will appear on screen when this movie is played.

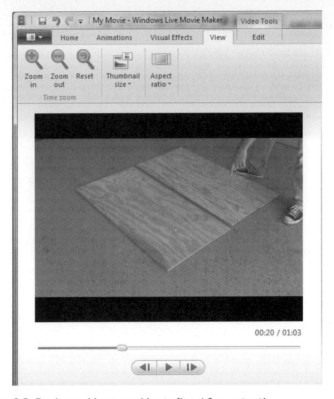

Figure 3-5. Forcing a widescreen video to fit a 4:3 aspect ratio.

ExplainED

There may be some instances where you will be playing your final movie on a specific television, flat screen, or other device (laptop) and wish to match the aspect ratio to the physical dimensions of the device showing your movie. In this instance, feel free to change the aspect ratio to match the display device.

Movie Maker is good at detecting the video you import and edit and determining the best aspect ratio to display it, but now you know how easy it is to change the aspect ratio when working with a mixture of videos that have been recorded using different ratios.

Rotating Video

I know the idea of rotating your video may sound strange. Most of us tend to shoot video by holding the video recorder vertically, because when we look through the eyehole or at the LCD screen of our camera, we see our subject(s) in the proper orientation. Most video recorders do not have the ability to detect when the device has been rotated (so that it's parallel to the ground) and then flip the recorded image for you. But there might be some instances where you need to shoot some footage by rotating your camera. Just keep in mind which aspect ratio you'll be using for your final movie. Rotating the camera will force whatever is on screen to be even smaller in detail, because the horizontal and vertical dimensions, which are swapped now, must fit a 4:3 or 16:9 display. This means Movie Maker will shrink the recorded image even more. (Just take a look at Figure 3-8 to see an example of what happens.)

Take a look at Figure 3-6. In this video, I had to rotate my camera so I could fit all the 2x4 pieces of wood into the image. If the image looks strange, it's because your eye and brain have that unique ability to take in the entire image and determine when something's not displayed correctly.

Figure 3-6. A video recorded at an odd angle will always be easily detected.

To fix this, I click the Home tab and then click the Rotate Left 90° button indicated in Figure 3-7 to rotate the image 90 degrees counter-clockwise.

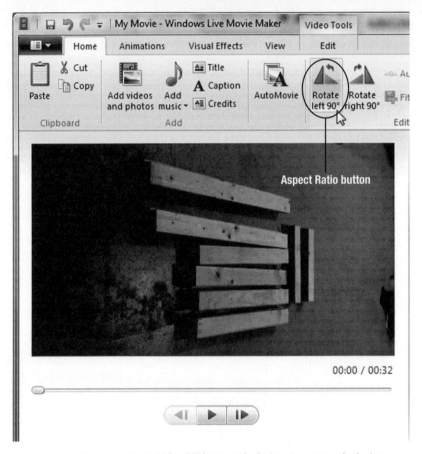

Figure 3-7. You can rotate a video 90 degrees clockwise or counter-clockwise.

After the video has been rotated, Figure 3-8 shows how the new video will be displayed on screen.

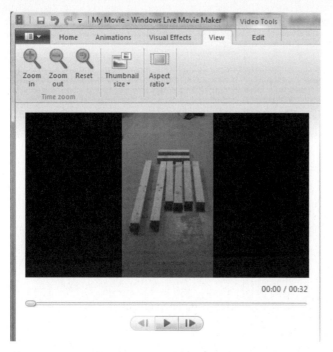

Figure 3-8. A rotated video will be forced to fit the default aspect ratio.

NotED

Would you ever want to rotate a video that already displays in the proper orientation? Of course! You've likely seen videos on the Internet or television that use a variety of special effects, including rotation. The rotation may simply be an artistic element to go along with music or to make a video more eye-catching. But be careful not to overdo it with the rotation. A little goes a long way.

Now the video looks right to my eyes (and hopefully to yours). But it's a little small, isn't it? Those vertical black bars have been added to the left and right so the rotated video will fit with the widescreen format that my video recorder used. Can I improve that?

In the previous section, I showed you how to change the aspect ratio. Let's see how it looks if I change it from 16:9 to 4:3. I choose the Standard (4:3) aspect ratio on the View tab. Figure 3-9 shows how the video will be displayed now.

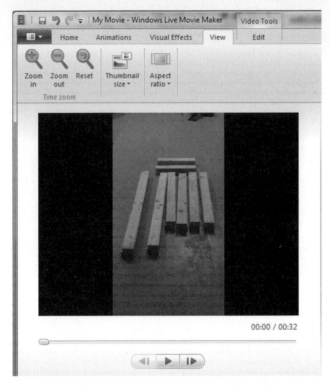

Figure 3-9. Changing the aspect ratio may improve a video's display size.

Not a huge improvement, but the video is definitely a little larger than the one shown in Figure 3-8. I think I'll leave this video at the 4:3 aspect ratio instead of the widescreen format.

ExplainED

My ultimate goal is to put together a DVD that I can share with friends that shows them how to build a worktable for themselves. The DVD will consist of many videos that I've edited (throughout the book), and I'll be creating a menu system so the viewer can select which video they wish to watch. The video displayed in Figure 3-9 will be a short video showing the 2x4 pieces after being cut. My goal is to provide the best videos, in the best format. The 4:3 format works for this rotated video, so I'll be keeping it.

Now that you know how to rotate a video, let me show you how to break a larger video into smaller videos.

Splitting a Video

At times you'll find yourself shooting video where you've let the camera continue to record rather than say "cut" between segments. What you'll end up with is a long video that contains some footage you wish to use, but with long (or short) pauses between the desired footage. There may be unwanted dialogue between you (the videographer) and your friend (the subject) as you tell him or her where to stand or how to make an entrance. For me, I have vacation video where there are long pauses between "action" where nothing is happening.

Before you do any cutting of video, you're likely to want to watch all of your video and make notes of what you wish to include in the final movie and what you wish to cut. Cutting scenes from a video is referred to as cropping. When you crop a video, you remove portions of it. But before I show you how to crop that unwanted footage (later in the "Trimming a Video" section), I'd like you to consider how easy it will be if you first break your longer videos into smaller, more manageable videos.

ExplainED

This splitting of videos isn't really trimming and editing away of unwanted footage: you'll use the Movie Maker trimming tools to do that. Instead, splitting a video makes it easier for you to break the footage into parts that can be individually edited later.

Take a look at Figure 3-10. It shows a video I've imported that is 51 seconds in length.

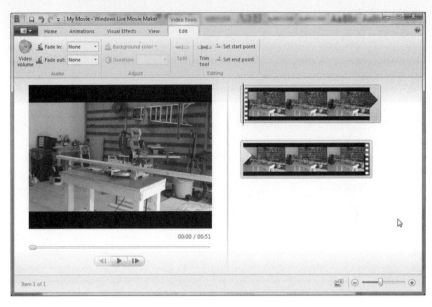

Figure 3-10. One long video is displayed using one continuous icon in the Library.

Notice that this single video is displayed as one continuous icon in the Library on the right-hand side of the screen. During this 51-second video, I left the camera running as I performed two tasks: finding and putting on my safety goggles, and finding and plugging in my extension cord. Both activities were done during those 51 seconds. Some of that footage I want to use, and some is unlikely to make it into the final video. But I'm not ready for trimming the video yet; instead, I'd like to break the one single video into two smaller videos, with each of the final two videos containing one of the two activities I just described.

Splitting this single video into two parts is simple with Movie Maker. To prepare for splitting the video, I will watch the complete video and make notes of the time displayed on the Video Timer in the lower right-hand corner of the Current Editing Section pane indicated in Figure 3-11. I will write down the time between each activity.

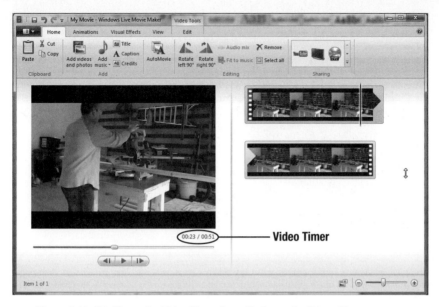

Figure 3-11. You'll use the Video Timer for splitting and editing videos.

Whether your long video contains two activities with a single break between them or ten activities with nine breaks between them, you'll use the video splitting tool the same way; just make a note of the time between each piece of footage you wish to turn into a single, smaller video. Write down the times with a description like this:

Finding and putting on Safety goggles

00:22 seconds – break

Finding and plugging in extension cord

00:51 seconds – end

Next, you'll use these times to easily and quickly split the bigger video. To do this, click and hold the black vertical line located in the larger video, as indicated in Figure 3-12.

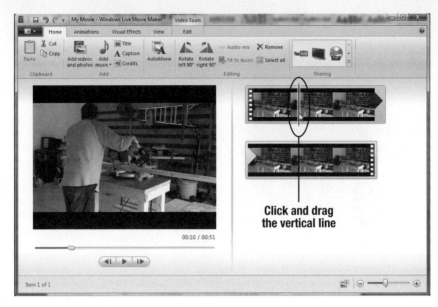

Figure 3-12. Splitting a video is done by using the vertical line.

As you drag the bar left or right, notice that the Video Timer changes. Simply drag the vertical line until the Video Timer shows the time you wrote down for the first split.

ExplainED

You can also use the Play, Pause, Rewind, and Fast Forward buttons. The vertical line will move along the video icon in the Library as the video plays.

Once the vertical line is located where the video will be split, simply click the *Split* button on the *Edit* tab as indicated in Figure 3-13.

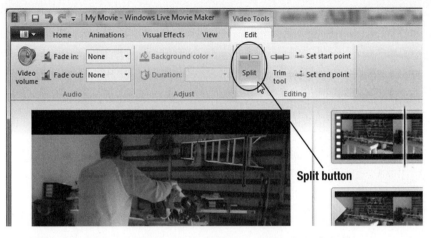

Figure 3-13. Click the Split button to divide your video where desired.

Now the single video is broken into two smaller videos. Figure 3-14 shows that I now have two icons in my Library pane. The first icon is the first 22 seconds of video, and the second icon is the remaining 29 seconds.

Figure 3-14. The single video is now broken into two parts.

NotED

When the video split is made, the point in time where you placed the vertical line for splitting isn't exact. Because Movie Maker doesn't allow you to split video by tenths or even hundredths of a second, the exact moment in time indicated by the Video Timer will be included in the latter (or second) video made by the split, not the former. Try to remember that, when splitting a video, anything seen onscreen will be included in video created after the split, not before.

If I wish to split the second video in Figure 3-14 into two smaller videos, I can simply drag the vertical bar to the location where I wish to split the video and perform the same actions just described. Movie Maker will allow you to split a two-second video into two one-second videos. You might find this useful for a quick montage of cut scenes for a fast-paced background song. The thing to remember is that you can keep dividing a larger video into smaller videos as much as you like.

As I mentioned earlier, the purpose of the split tool is to divide larger videos into smaller, more manageable ones. These smaller videos are faster for you to view, edit, and work on than one long video. Because you can select a video in the Library when you wish to edit or add special effects, you'll find it is much more efficient to spend the time necessary splitting your large videos into smaller ones. This will become much more apparent when you begin the process of trimming your videos.

Trimming a Video

You've now learned how to change the aspect ratio of an imported video, how to rotate that video (if necessary), and how to split a longer video into one or more smaller videos. At this point, you should have one or more videos that are now ready for some trimming and cutting.

Trimming a video is just what it sounds like: removing bits and pieces of footage from a video to cut its length down. Trimming a video is simple, but let me first explain how to make the best cuts.

ExplainED

Are you remembering to work only from a copy of the raw video files? Any splits or rotations that you've added will be saved in the video file stored on your hard drive. That's why it's important to always work from a copy of your raw video files; if you find that you've made a mistake with rotating, splitting, or trimming a video, you can always go back to the original raw video and start over.

For all videos that you work with, there is a starting point and an ending point. For the 51-second video that I split into two parts, the start of the movie (in Figure 3-11) is still 00:00, and the end of the movie is 00:51. The movie consists of all the videos (and photos) in the Library, one running right after another. (Photos, by default, run for five seconds, but you can change this. I show you how to do so in Chapter 5.)

Remember that you can drag and drop videos and photos in the Library to reorder them. Figure 3-15 shows me dragging the second video (from Figure 3-14) to the beginning of the Library. Note that this doesn't change the length of the movie: it is still 51 seconds in length. It just changes the order in which the activities are performed. (In this case, I'm finding the extension cord and *then* finding and putting on my safety goggles.) I'll return the videos to their original order.

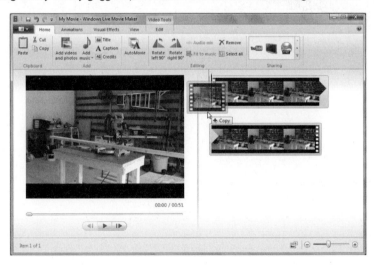

Figure 3-15. Reordering videos doesn't change the length of the final movie.

NotED

By reordering my videos in Figure 3-15, I've introduced what is known in the film world as a "continuity problem." When I split the video, the first half of the total movie showed me finding and locating my safety goggles before finding the extension cord. But after dragging the second half of the video to the front, anyone watching the movie will see me wearing my safety goggles as I find the extension cord, and then finding and putting on my safety goggles in the next scene. But wait, wasn't I just wearing them? That's a continuity problem: accidentally reordering a video so a timeline problem is readily apparent to the viewer. Be careful about making these! How strange would it be to show your in-laws a video of their grandson playing with his new toy and then the video jumps to show him opening the wrapped box containing the toy?

Remember, simply reordering the videos and photos in the Library doesn't change the overall length of the movie. Only after you begin trimming away excess and unwanted footage from your videos will the total length of the movie decrease.

To trim, you'll once again be viewing each individual video in your library and making note of the starting time of the footage you want to keep, as well as the ending time.

I'll return to the two videos I created by splitting a long video. In the first video, I'm finding and putting on my safety goggles. In the second video, I'm finding my extension cable hanging on the wall. During both of those videos, there are a few seconds here and there that are, to me, unwanted footage. I'll start with the first video by clicking at its starting point, as shown in Figure 3-16.

Figure 3-16. Start the trimming process by selecting a video for editing.

This video is 22 seconds in length, but I don't make an appearance until seven seconds into the video, as you can see in Figure 3-17.

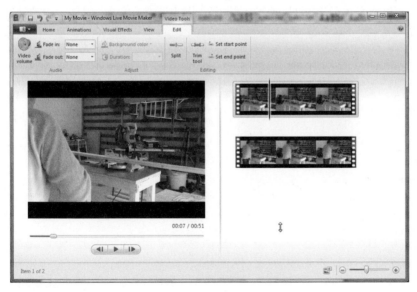

Figure 3-17. The first six seconds are unwanted footage.

To begin the trimming, I drag the black vertical bar (the same one used for splitting a video) to the seven-second mark (where I first appear), and click the *Set Start Point* button indicated in Figure 3-18.

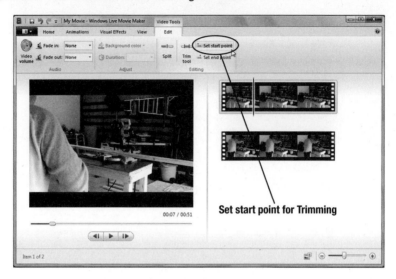

Set start point for Trimming

Figure 3-18. Set the start point for the trimming action.

Figure 3-19 shows what happens next. Notice that the total length of the movie has changed from 00:51 seconds to 00:44 seconds. You can also see that the icon representing the first half of the movie has shortened a bit. I've trimmed my movie!

But I'm not done yet. When I press the Play button and watch the newly trimmed first video, I find that after I've placed my safety goggles on there are a couple of seconds of unwanted footage. This begins at the 00:14 seconds mark, as shown in Figure 3-20.

Figure 3-19. The overall length of the movie has been shortened.

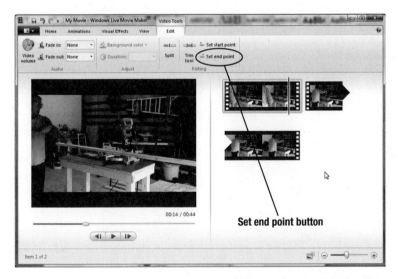

Figure 3-20. Set an end point to trim unwanted footage from the end of a video.

Move the vertical line to that point and click the *Set End Point* button indicated in Figure 3-20. The last few seconds are removed, and I can once again see that the movie's length has shortened to 00:41 seconds, as shown in Figure 3-21.

Figure 3-21. The movie's length changes to reflect the start and end point trims.

But I'm still not done yet. If I don't like my start or end point selections, I can use the *Undo* command (or click Ctrl-Z) to undo any of the edits I've made. If I'm satisfied with the trimming, only one task remains. I click the *Trim Tool* button indicated in Figure 3-22.

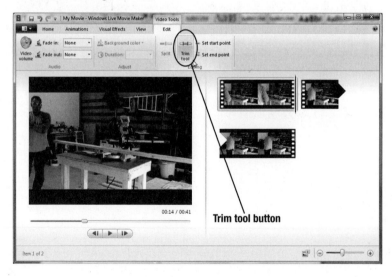

Trim tool button

Figure 3-22. The Trim Tool button is used to cut away unwanted footage.

The screen shown in Figure 3-23 appears.

Figure 3-23. Be sure to save your project so you won't lose any of your work.

You are shown the video that will remain after your trims are made. You can press the Play, Rewind, and Fast Forward buttons to view your edits before finalizing them. You can also fine-tune the starting and ending trim points, down to hundredths of a second. Use the Up and Down arrows indicated in Figure 3-23 to fine-tune your cuts. Click the *Save Trim* button to trim the video, or the *Cancel* button to return to the untrimmed video to start over.

I'll click the *Save Trim* button. Figure 3-24 shows my movie with newly trimmed first video cut down a bit in length.

Figure 3-24. The first video is trimmed from 22 seconds to 14 seconds.

I'll perform the same trimming actions on the second video. In that video, I hunt down and remove my extension cable from the wall, but there are quite a few seconds at the beginning and end that are just not needed. After making the trims, I was able to cut the original 51 seconds video down to 25 seconds, as shown in Figure 3-25.

I've managed to cut the original movie length by more than 50 percent. This means my viewers have less to watch, but it also means they don't have to suffer through watching a lot of footage in which nothing is happening and I'm just wandering around.

Figure 3-25. The final movie is trimmed from 51 seconds to 25 seconds.

NotED

Another benefit to the trimming is it cuts the videos down in terms of file size. Every megabyte counts, and if you intend to share your videos via email or an online service like YouTube, you're going to find that the smaller the video is in length, the smaller it will be in size. Your viewers will appreciate your trimming work!

Trimming your videos is a skill that improves with practice. Always remember that the purpose of trimming your videos is to make your final movie more enjoyable and entertaining. Use trimming with care, but do use it. Keep your audience in mind as you cut away excess footage, and always ask yourself if the footage in question will make your final movie a better experience for the viewer.

What's Next?

Editing a movie for length and content is just one part of the equation. Entertaining your viewer is also important, and one way to do that is to provide music or commentary with your videos. Some videos will require a voiceover to explain what is being viewed. Some video may be self-explanatory, but lack any sound or dialogue. Whatever the case, Movie Maker gives you the ability to make your videos shine by including music and commentary, and Chapter 4 will get you started on the blending of audio and video.

Chapter 4

Working with Audio

Back in the early days of movies, silent films were immensely popular. For the first time in history, people could watch moving images rather than just still photo images. To make up for the lack of sound, a pianist or guitarist would occasionally be hired to provide accompanying music to go along with the action. Dialogue was provided using text that was inserted into the movie; the limitation of the screen size, however, usually meant that the text had to be short in length. A drawback was that this limited the amount of information the viewer could receive. Still, it was a start.

Today's movies would completely shock those early silent film moviegoers. Sound is an often-overlooked feature of movies, because most of us have never known movies without dialogue, sound effects, and music. But take away sound, and today's audience would be in an uproar.

In addition to being able to edit your movies, Movie Maker also provides the capability to import music and other sounds. From voice-overs to humorous sound effects (BOI-OI-OI-ING!), you have the ability to provide your movies with a little extra BAM! or KaPOW! Or maybe you'd just like to put a very light piano rendition of a classical tune running along with your movie's action.

Whatever your needs, I'm going to show you in this chapter just how easy it is to bring sound to your movies with Movie Maker.

Varieties of Sound

I can't predict all the possible ways you may want to use sound to enhance your movies. But I can safely suggest a few that are fairly standard and are found in most movies. After explaining what these three options are, I'll show you how to use Movie Maker to implement all of them.

Background Music

We're all familiar with background music. It's the song or tune that's playing, sometimes quietly and sometimes loudly, with the action on the screen. If you're watching a video of two motorcyclists racing, it's likely the music playing is a fast-tempo, high-volume, rock-and-roll song. On the other hand, a video of a couple walking quietly down the streets of Paris is probably going to be accompanied by a soft jazz tune or some classical music.

This isn't to say that music can't be used to unbalance the viewer; mismatched music has been used by many professional movie directors to make a scene more dramatic or comedic. The key is to match the music with the emotion you wish the movie watcher to experience.

Background music is also often playing lightly in order to not overwhelm other sounds that are being generated, such as dialogue. It can be frustrating to try and listen to one or more people talking in a movie if the background music is too loud. Sounds that are important to a scene, such as a baby cooing, a wolf howling in the distance, or a car's engine running, can easily be missed by including background music that's too loud or too fast.

Remember, though: some scenes just don't need music. Music is great, but sometimes it's overkill. If your scene has a lot of talking between multiple people, adding music may make it difficult for the viewer to understand all or parts of the conversation. Video of a sporting event may include a sportscaster in the background; adding music may prevent you from hearing the play-by-play announcements. Ultimately, it will be your decision on when to use music and when to not use it.

Now, if you've chosen to include some background music with a video, you're probably wondering how to add it in to the video. I'm happy to tell you that it's extremely simple. Figure 4-1 shows Movie Maker open with five short videos (previously trimmed in Chapter 3) loaded into the Library.

Figure 4-1. These five small videos will make up one long 40-second movie.

These five short videos are all between 7 and 15 seconds in length. But combined, the movie is 40 seconds long. There's not a lot happening in these videos in terms of dialogue (I'm not talking) or background sounds (just the sound of the saw cutting), so some background music would be great!

This brings up a question, though. Do I wish to have the background music playing across one of the smaller videos or across the entire 40-second movie? The good news is that both options are available. I'm going to show you how to do both, but first I need to show you how to import your music.

LinkED

Legally, you cannot use a copyrighted song in your movie if you're going to share it with anyone else. You have to pay a fee to do this, and it's beyond the scope of this book to discuss the legal intricacies of the music industry. If your movie will be distributed, given away, or in any way used in a money-making manner, I highly recommend consulting with an attorney. The consequences can be very expensive.

Start by clicking the Add Music button, as shown in Figure 4-2.

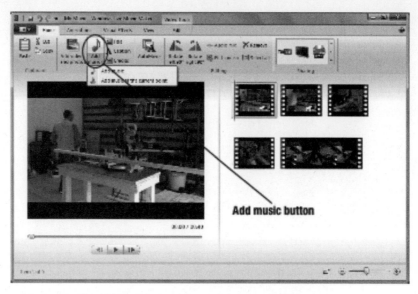

Figure 4-2. The Add Music button allows you to import songs.

You have two options available from the drop-down menu shown in Figure 4-2: Add Music and Add Music At the Current Point. For now, I'm going to select Add Music; Figure 4-3 shows the screen that appears.

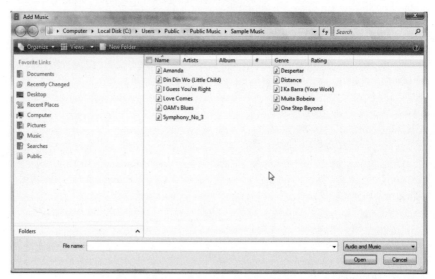

Figure 4-3. Browse and select any song or sound effect stored on your hard drive.

You'll need to browse your hard drive and locate the song you wish to use. I've selected "Symphony No. 3" and clicked the *Open* button. Figure 4-4 shows how Movie Maker displays the song spread out over the entire movie.

The song and it's length

Figure 4-4. A box is added above the videos to indicate a song is playing.

As you can see, the song is playing over the entire 40-second video. This is indicated by the boxes sitting above the individual videos' icons in the Library. Go ahead and click the Play button and watch: as your movie plays, the music will play in the background.

LinkED

You can download "Symphony #3" and the five videos so you can follow along. Just visit the book page at www.friendsofed.com and download the Chapter 4 files.

After adding the music, I noticed two problems. First, the actual noises I'm making in the video (cutting the wood) are louder than the music. Second, the song starts and ends with no fade-in or fade-out; when the movie ends, the song abruptly stops. This can be fixed.

First, let's fix the lack of a fade-in and fade-out. Double-click anywhere on the song in the Library. Figure 4-5 shows how Movie Maker opens a *Music Tools* tab.

Figure 4-5. The Music Tools tab allows you to edit a song.

For both the Fade-In and Fade-Out, you can choose from Slow, Medium, or Fast speeds as shown in Figure 4-6. You can always go back and change the speed to None at a later time. (I've currently selected a Slow Fade-in and a Medium Fade-Out).

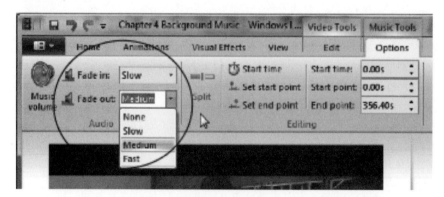

Figure 4-6. Fade-in and Fade-out options are added with a single click.

Now play your movie and listen. Did you hear the fade-in and fade-out? Feel free to go back and increase or decrease the speed until it suits you.

Before I leave this screen, let me point out a few other options available to you. First, you can increase or decrease the sound of the background music by clicking the *Music Volume* button indicated in Figure 4-7. A slider bar appears that you can click and drag left or right to increase or decrease the volume. (But remember, this is not the volume of the video; this controls the volume of the song you imported. I'll show you shortly how to control the volume of video itself.)

Figure 4-7. Increase or decrease the background volume using the slider.

Other features on the *Music Tools* tab include the ability to specify the exact location in a video where you wish the music to start and end. When I imported the song earlier, I didn't specify a specific spot in the movie (by using the other option, Add Music At the Current Point), so the song was placed so it would start at the same time as the first video and end when the last video was over.

Figure 4-8 shows that I can tweak the music by changing different values using three controls: *Start Time*, *Start Point*, and *End Point*.

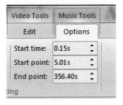

Figure 4-8. You can control when the music starts and where in the music to begin.

The Start time control simply lets you specify at what point in time (in seconds) that you wish the music to begin. Click the up and down arrows to increase or decrease the time.

The Start point is a bit different, however. Let's say your song is two minutes in length (120 seconds). If the first 10 or 15 seconds of the song are not something you wish to have playing, you can simply set the Start Point to 15.00s, and when your movie begins, the first 15 seconds of the song will be ignored and the video will immediately play with the music at the 15s mark playing. This is perfect for matching that exact point in a favorite song with the video you wish to match it to.

The End Point works the same way; set the time in seconds, not minutes, for where you wish the song to end. If the snippet of song that you've chosen is shorter than the length of the video (or entire movie), then the song will simply end at the configured time, and any remaining time left in the movie will play without background music. Just keep in mind that you're not cropping the music; the entire song will still be available for you to make changes. This will allow you to fine-tune your song and video to start together and make the strongest impact.

NotED

Where can you obtain music that is legal to use for your movies? There are a lot of songs available that are in the public domain; that is, they're free to use in any manner you like. Just do an Internet search for "public domain music" and you'll find tons of Web sites that offer free music for downloading.

Now that you've learned how to control the volume, starting point, and end points of songs, let me finish up by showing you how to reduce the volume of your video so the background music is easier heard.

Start by clicking the *Edit* tab, and then one of your videos. Figure 4-9 shows that I've selected the second video in my Library; in that video, I'm cutting a piece of 2 × 4 and the saw is quite loud! Click the *Video Volume* button and you'll see a slider similar to the one for the *Music Volume*.

Figure 4-9. The Edit tab will let you change the video volume.

Drag the slider left or right to decrease or increase the video's volume. You'll likely have to experiment and change this a few times to find the perfect balance of video volume and background music volume.

Do note that you'll need to change the video volume for each video in your library. The video volume you select for one video will not be changed in all other videos.

And that's how you add music to a video, a collection of videos, or an entire movie. Not too difficult, is it? If you wish to add more music to your movie, simply perform the same import action, but this time, the next song you import will be added to the end of the previous song, no matter where that song may end. Notice in Figure 4-10 that I specified that "Symphony #3" end at the 30-second mark.

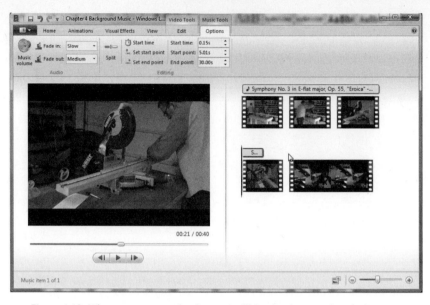

Figure 4-10. Where one song ends, the next will begin when you import it.

Now, if I import the song "Despertar," it will start right where "Symphony #3" ends, as seen in Figure 4-11.

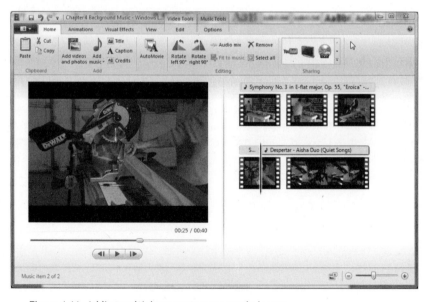

Figure 4-11. Adding multiple songs to your movie is easy.

Of course, it's now up to you to use what you've learned about fade-ins, fade-outs, and starting and ending points to edit the imported music to match the video. But as you can see, you've got some great tools to control when, where, and at what volume your music plays.

Sound Effects

Music is great for spans of video, but what about short and quick sound effects? Would your movie's viewers enjoy an occasional funny sound effect or some sort of exaggerated sound added to an appropriate moment in your movie?

Well, you'll be happy to know that adding a sound effect is just as easy as adding and editing background music. Just think of a sound effect as a half-second song and I think you'll understand how this works.

In my second video in Figure 4-11, after I cut the 2 × 4 in half, one half of it falls to the ground with a loud bang. I'd like to change that to the sound of breaking glass. Here's how I'll do it.

First, you need to find a sound effect. You can record it yourself (using the steps I'll cover in the next section on creating voice-overs) or find it on the Internet. I've found a very short but funny sound of breaking glass and downloaded it to my hard drive.

Now I need to insert this sound effect at the point where the board falls. Figure 4-12 shows that I've located that exact point; the vertical black line indicates where in the video I wish to insert the sound effect.

Now, something unusual has happened. Figure 4-13 shows the new glass sound effect has been added, but in doing so it ended "Symphony #3" and the second song, "OAM Blues," immediately starts. This is one of the limitations of Movie Maker; it can only play one imported song (or sound effect) at a particular point in a video. You can either have a song or a sound effect, but not both. To fix this problem, simply click the existing song ("Symphony #3," in this instance) and click the Split button on the Edit tab, as shown in Figure 4-13.

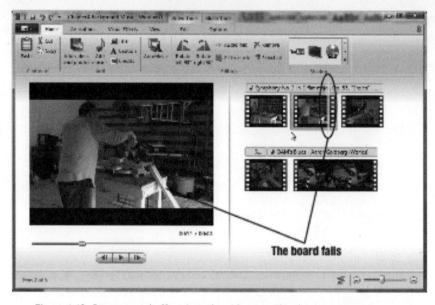

Figure 4-12. Drop a sound effect into the video exactly where you want it.

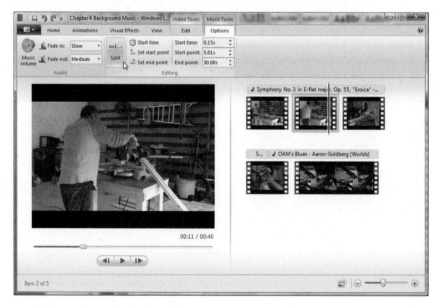

Figure 4-13. Use the Split button to break a song in two.

The song will be split and you can insert your sound effect without worrying that your song will be removed; this is shown in Figure 4-14. After the sound effect plays, the background music will keep playing at the point where it was temporarily stopped.

Figure 4-14. Insert your sound effect between a split song.

Once you have your sound effect added to the video, you can double-click it and edit its volume and start point just like editing an imported song. This is how you can tweak your sound effect to get it to trigger at exactly the right point in your movie.

NotED

Another option for adding sound effects over background music is to use third-party software such as Audacity (http://audacity.sourceforge.net) that will allow you to merge a song with a sound effect. What you're really doing is embedding the sound effect in the song first, and then importing the newly merged song/sound effect into Movie Maker.

As with all things, special sound effects should be used with care and in limited quantity. Too many humorous sound effects can get annoying quickly, so don't overuse them.

Voice-overs

Have you ever watched a video and had difficulty understanding what was going on in the scene, or maybe what you were looking at? I watched a friend's video a while back of his tour of a museum; it had some great shots of some amazing exhibits, but I had no idea what I was looking at from scene to scene. In a few instances, he would talk about whatever it was he was shooting, but his voice was hard to hear over the voices of the other exhibit visitors and the random noises you generally encounter in public places (babies crying, phones ringing, and so on).

What his video lacked was a voice-over. A voice-over is a recorded narration (by you or someone else) that is added to a video, just like a song. You've heard voice-overs used in commercials and documentaries, so you likely understand how they work. The narrator is simply providing audible information about whatever is being seen on the screen, whether it's vacation footage, a baby's first steps, or building a workbench that involves a lot of cutting and drilling.

In this final section, I want to show you how easy it is to help your viewers make sense of certain points in your movie that may otherwise be confusing. And, just like sound effects, think of a voice-over as background music when it comes to importing, editing, and starting and stopping points. The only difference between a voice-over and a song is that you're going to need to create the voiceover by recording it first.

ExplainED

It will be easier for you to use voice-overs if you break them up into smaller bits. If you have a five-minute movie, rather than create one long five-minute sound file, consider breaking it up into smaller sound files. Doing so will help you when it comes time to place the voiceover sound files in specific spots. It will also be extremely helpful if you ever choose to rearrange videos in your movie; you won't have to re-record a voiceover with the changes. Instead, you'll simply reorganize the smaller sound files.

To show you how this works, I'm going to create a five-second voice-over for the very first video shown in Figure 4-1. In that video, all I'm doing is locating my safety goggles. It's fairly boring, so I'm going to add a simple voice-over that says, "It all starts with the safety goggles."

All versions of Windows come with the Sound Recorder application. You'll find it in the Accessories folder under the Start button. Locate and open Sound Recorder and you'll see it open as shown in Figure 4-15.

Figure 4-15. The Sound Recorder is a simple looking application.

The Sound Recorder has a simple interface. Just click the Record button (indicated by the red dot) and start talking. (If your computer doesn't have a built-in microphone, you will need to connect an external microphone to your computer's microphone port.)

When you're done recording, click the Stop button and a window will open, like the one in Figure 4-16, where you can save the sound file.

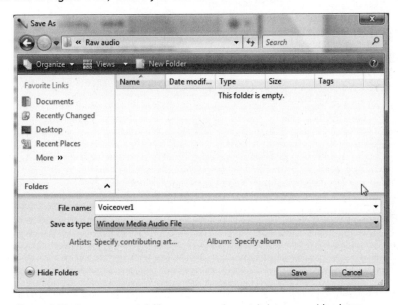

Figure 4-16. Save your sound file so you can import it into your video later.

ExplainED

I create a "Raw audio" folder in Chapter 2 where I can store my original sound recordings. Remember to always work with a copy of your sound files so you won't accidentally delete or trim the originals.

Figure 4-17 shows that I've imported the voiceover1 sound file and placed it at the beginning of the very first video.

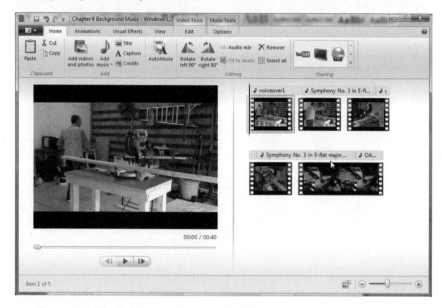

Figure 4-17. The first 6 seconds are unwanted footage.

Don't worry about editing your recordings; you can actually do this from within Movie Maker! Simple double-click the voice-over sound file and you'll be given the same editing tools available for music editing, as seen in Figure 4-18.

86

Figure 4-18. Set the start point for the trimming action.

You can do the same thing with voice-over sound files as with any sound file. You can increase or decrease the volume, set its starting point in time, even split it! If you find, for example, that your voiceover would be better as two separate sound files, simply split it using the *Split* button. After splitting it, you can fine-tune the starting and ending points of both new sound files. Simple!

NotED

Sound Recorder is a simple application with no bells and whistles. If you desire more professional results from your voice-overs, you're going to want to use third-party applications such as Audacity (audacity.sourceforge.net) for more editing power.

What's Next?

Now that you know how to edit both sound and video, it's time to start adding in some visual special effects. These special effects will add some unique visual elements to your movie, and help separate your videos from those simple (and boring) straight recordings that we have all been forced to watch. Special effects take your movies to a slightly higher level, but they can be overused and become annoying to your viewers. In Chapter 5, I'm going to explain the first type of special effects, called animations, and how to use them properly.

Chapter 5

Working with Animations

If you've ever watched any homemade movies, this scenario might be familiar:

Uncle Ned presses play on the DVD player. The video immediately displays a large group of people standing around in what appears to be a large building. The sound is horrible because the video recorder's microphone is picking up on hundreds of conversations. The scene jumps to a close-up of a very old book. (Uncle Ned pauses the video and tells you, "This is our visit to the Sistine Chapel.") After a few seconds the video jumps to Aunt Matilda standing next to a group of ladies you don't recognize. The scene changes quickly to show the ceiling of the chapel. The scene changes again to show a few quick close-ups of various historic and valuable artifacts that you're not familiar with, and then changes quickly again to show you five or six quick scenes of various walls and displays around the chapel.

Are you completely and utterly disinterested? Me, too. I already know that this movie needs some serious editing and maybe some voice-overs (which I covered in Chapter 4), but even if Uncle Ned took the time to trim out some of the scenes that aren't too useful (ladies standing around?), the scenes jump abruptly from one to the next. It's giving me a headache. What this movie needs is some more subtle transitions from one scene to the next.

Fortunately, Movie Maker provides the ability to add these transitions. They're called animations, and they give you the ability to ease your viewers from one scene to the next. They can be applied to video and photographs, so it's easy to create home movies that don't have that jarring effect on viewers.

But just like any type of special effect (such as video and sound), you can overwhelm your viewers by overusing these types of transitions. You've probably heard the phrase "less is more," and it really does apply with animations. That said, you can really put the power of animations to work and make your movies stand out with some powerful transition techniques.

I'm going to start this chapter by introducing you to the various animations that are available, and then show you how to implement them in your own movies. I'll also be offering up some advice on how to use animations properly so they don't overwhelm or confuse the viewer. Let's take a look.

Types of Animations

In Movie Maker, there are many types of animations: dissolves, reveals, and shatters are just a few. I'll be going over all of them shortly, but for now I'd like you to take a look at Figure 5-1. This figure shows a handful of videos that I'm currently working on. These videos have already been edited by removing unwanted scenes and actions.

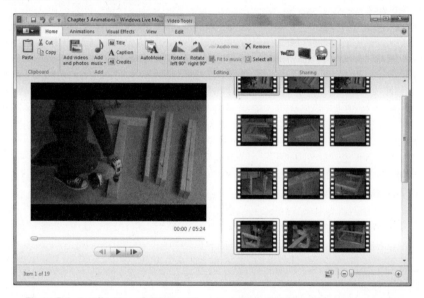

Figure 5-1. A collection of videos with no transitions between them.

All of these videos are short (between 5 and 20 seconds), and they show me building my workbench frame. The short videos are in order, from start to finish, and the entire movie is 5 minutes and 24 seconds in length. While I could easily leave the movie as it is, watching it jump from scene to scene is a little boring and, quite honestly, a bit annoying. What I want to do is use these Dissolves and Reveals to engage my viewer and increase his or her interest in what the videos are displaying. (I'll go back and add voice-overs and music after I've added in my animations. Refer to Chapter 4 for instructions on adding music and voice-overs.)

To work with animations, you'll start by clicking the *Animations* tab, as shown in Figure 5-2.

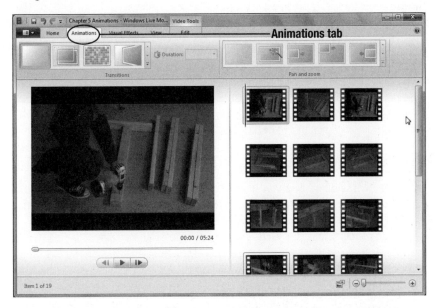

Figure 5-2. The Animations tab is where you find a variety of movie transitions.

Rather than explain what an animation is, it's easier to just show you. Open Movie Maker, import a few videos, and click the *Animations* tab. After the *Animations* tab is selected, click the *Transitions* "More" button, as indicated in Figure 5-3.

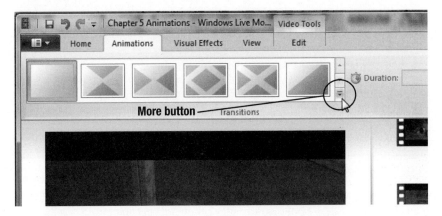

Figure 5-3. The More button gives you access to different animations.

After clicking the More button, you'll see a drop-down menu like the one shown in Figure 5-4.

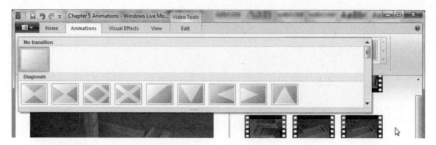

Figure 5-4. In the drop-down menu, the animations are broken into categories.

Scroll down this menu and you'll see a total of eight different categories: No Transition, Diagonals, Dissolves, Patterns & Shapes, Reveals, Shatters, Sweeps & Curls, and Wipes. Each category (with the exception of No Transition) has a collection of icons that represent a different type of animation.

ExplainED

Some of the icons are fairly easy to figure out, but not all of them. Unfortunately, the only real way to see an animation at work is to simply select it and try it. Movie Maker does provide a preview of each animation, so you'll be able to see what it does without actually selecting it for a video.

To add an animation to a video, you simply select the video in your Library, click the *Animations* tab's More button, scroll through the categories, and pick an animation you wish to use. Hovering your mouse over an animation will give you a quick 2-3 second preview in the Editing screen, as shown in Figure 5-5.

In Figure 5-5, I selected the "Diagonal - box out" animation; it adds an animation between the video selected and the one preceding it. This is important. Always remember that animations are added to the beginning of a selected video, so the animation will be inserted between the selected video and the one in front of it. Figure 5-6 shows the small triangle icon that's added to a video to indicate a transition is present.

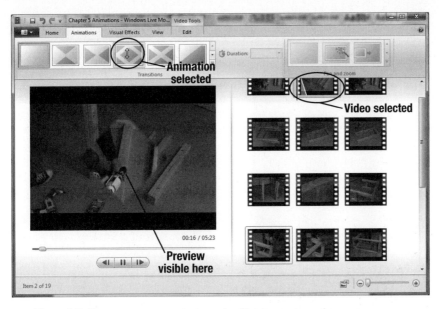

Figure 5-5. Hover your mouse over an animation to see a preview.

Figure 5-6. Fade-in and Fade-out options are added with a single click.

To remove an animation, simply click the video with the triangle icon and select the No Transition option from the More button's drop-down menu (refer to Figure 5-4).

Now that you know how to add a transition and remove one, let me go over the various types of animations and how they appear on the screen.

NotED

The first video in your movie will have a limited number of animations available to it. Because it's the first video, there's no video before it to transition from, right? Movie Maker gives you only three animation options for the opening scene of a movie: Crossfade, Pixelate, or Flip. I'll cover these three options in their respective categories below.

Diagonals

The Diagonals category offers a total of nine different animations. The icon and name of each animation appear in Figure 5-7, along with a brief explanation of the animation's visual activity.

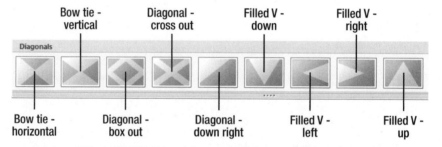

Figure 5-7. All nine animation icons for the Diagonals category.

Bow Tie - Horizontal

The "Bow tie - horizontal" animation adds a transition from Video 1 to Video 2 using a bow-tie-shaped animation that grows from the left and right edges of Video 1 to Video 2. Scenes from Video 2 are visible in the bow tie as it grows larger.

BowTie - Vertical

The "Bow tie - vertical" animation adds a transition from Video 1 to Video 2 using a bow-tie-shaped animation that grows from the top and bottom edges of Video 1 to Video 2. Scenes from Video 2 are visible in the bow tie as it grows larger.

Diagonal - Box Out

The "Diagonal – box out" animation adds a transition from Video 1 to Video 2 using a diamond-shaped box animation that shrinks from the center of Video 1.

Scenes from Video 2 are visible in the surrounding areas as the diamond shrinks.

Diagonal – Cross Out

The "Diagonal – cross out" animation adds a transition from Video 1 to Video 2 using an X-shaped pattern animation that grows from the center of Video 1. Scenes from Video 2 are visible in the X-shaped pattern areas as it grows.

Diagonal – Down Right

The "Diagonal – down right" animation adds a transition from Video 1 to Video 2 using an animation that moves diagonally from the upper left-hand corner of Video 1 to the lower right-hand corner. Like a page being turned, scenes from Video 2 are visible beginning in the upper left-hand corner and completely visible when the animation reaches the lower right-hand corner of the screen.

Filled V Down

The "Filled V down" animation adds a transition from Video 1 to Video 2 using a V-shaped block animation that moves from the top of the screen to the bottom. Scenes from Video 2 are visible in the V-shaped block as it grows.

Filled V Left

The "Filled V left" animation adds a transition from Video 1 to Video 2 using a V-shaped block animation that moves from the right edge of Video 1 to the left edge. Scenes from Video 2 are visible in the V-shaped block as it grows.

Filled V Right

The "Filled V right" animation adds a transition from Video 1 to Video 2 using a V-shaped block animation that moves from the left edge of Video 1 to the right edge. Scenes from Video 2 are visible in the V-shaped block as it grows.

Filled V Up

The "Filled V up" animation adds a transition from Video 1 to Video 2 using a V-shaped block animation that moves from the bottom of the screen to the top. Scenes from Video 2 are visible in the V-shaped block as it grows.

Dissolves

The Dissolves category offers a total of six different animations. The icon and name of each animation appear in Figure 5-8, along with a brief explanation of the animation's visual activity.

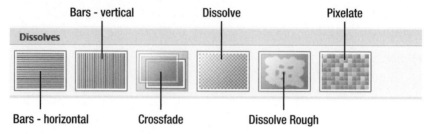

Figure 5-8. All six animation icons for the Dissolves category.

Bars - Horizontal

The "Bars – horizontal" animation adds a transition from Video 1 to Video 2 using a series of thin, random horizontal lines. Scenes from Video 1 are "overwritten" as more lines are added to the screen. Each horizontal line contains a sliver of the scene from Video 2.

Bars - Vertical

The "Bars – vertical" animation adds a transition from Video 1 to Video 2 using a series of thin, random vertical lines. Scenes from Video 1 are "overwritten" as more lines are added to the screen. Each vertical line contains a sliver of the scene from Video 2.

Crossfade

The Crossfade animation adds a transition from Video 1 to Video 2 that blends scenes from both videos evenly. The effect is a fade-out of Video 1 and a fade-in of Video 2.

Dissolve

The Dissolve animation adds a transition from Video 1 to Video 2 that is similar to the Crossfade animation, but uses larger pixel blocks for the fade-in and fade-out effect.

Dissolve Rough

The "Dissolve rough" animation adds a transition from Video 1 to Video 2 that is similar to the Dissolve animation, but uses a "liquid" pattern versus a pixel pattern. The effect is a covering of Video 1 with the "spilling" of Video 2 over it.

Pixelate

The Pixelate animation adds a transition from Video 1 to Video 2 that is similar to the Dissolve animation, but uses much larger pixels to blur out Video 1 and fade-in with scenes from Video 2.

Patterns & Shapes

The "Patterns & shapes" category offers a total of 11 different animations. The icon and name of each animation appear in Figure 5-9, along with a brief explanation of the animation's visual activity.

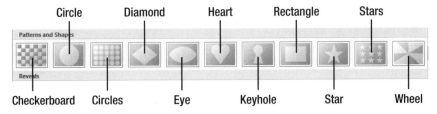

Figure 5-9. All 11 animation icons for the Patterns & Shapes category.

NotED

Patterns are fun to play with. Shapes, such as the heart, are perfect transitions for wedding videos, for example. The keyhole pattern could be fun for a house tour video or maybe a walkthrough of a museum. Creative uses of the shapes are limited to your imagination.

Checkerboard

The Checkerboard animation adds a transition from Video 1 to Video 2 that replaces the scene from Video 1 by overwriting it with a pattern of small squares. As the squares are drawn on the screen, each square contains a small bit of the scene from Video 2.

Circle

The Circle animation adds a transition from Video 1 to Video 2 that replaces the scene from Video 1 by overwriting it with a growing circle that starts in the center of the screen. The scene from Video 2 is contained in the enlarging circle.

Circles

The Circles animation adds a transition from Video 1 to Video 2 that replaces the scene from Video 1 by overwriting it with a series of growing circles that are evenly spaced on the screen. The scene from Video 2 is contained in the enlarging circles.

Diamond

The Diamond animation adds a transition from Video 1 to Video 2 that replaces the scene from Video 1 by overwriting it with a growing diamond that starts in the center of the screen. The scene from Video 2 is contained in the enlarging diamond.

Eye

The Eye animation adds a transition from Video 1 to Video 2 that replaces the scene from Video 1 by overwriting it with a growing eye-shaped block that starts in the center of the screen. The scene from Video 2 is contained in the enlarging block.

Heart

The Heart animation adds a transition from Video 1 to Video 2 that replaces the scene from Video 1 by overwriting it with a growing heart-shaped block that starts in the center of the screen. The scene from Video 2 is contained in the enlarging block.

Keyhole

The Keyhole animation adds a transition from Video 1 to Video 2 that replaces the scene from Video 1 by overwriting it with a growing keyhole-shaped block that starts in the center of the screen. The scene from Video 2 is contained in the enlarging block.

Rectangle

The Rectangle animation adds a transition from Video 1 to Video 2 that replaces the scene from Video 1 by overwriting it with a growing rectangle that starts in the center of the screen. The scene from Video 2 is contained in the enlarging rectangle.

Star

The Star animation adds a transition from Video 1 to Video 2 that replaces the scene from Video 1 by overwriting it with a growing star that starts in the center of the screen. The scene from Video 2 is contained in the enlarging star.

Stars

The Stars animation adds a transition from Video 1 to Video 2 that replaces the scene from Video 1 by overwriting it with a series of growing stars that are evenly spaced on the screen. The scene from Video 2 is contained in the enlarging stars.

Wheel

The Wheel animation adds a transition from Video 1 to Video 2 that replaces the scene from Video 1 by overwriting it with animation similar to a spinning pinwheel. The scene from Video 2 is contained in the spinning portion of the animation.

Reveals

The Reveals category offers a total of 15 different animations: the largest category of animations. The icon and name of each animation appear in Figure 5-10, along with a brief explanation of the animation's visual activity.

Flip

The Flip animation adds a transition from Video 1 to Video 2 that replaces the scene from Video 1 by "flipping" it over. The effect is displayed as if Video 2 is running on the backside of Video 1.

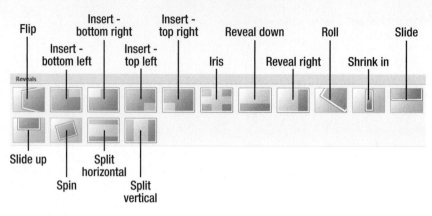

Figure 5-10. All 15 animation icons for the Reveals category.

NotED

Reveals are fun, but they are best used in limited quantity and with few changes between their motions. I suggest using the same reveal as often as possible. It's less annoying to viewers, and is a visual clue to a change in scene or subject. If you are going to select multiple reveals, consider using opposites. Flipping back and forth between Insert-Bottom Right and Insert Top Right can provide just enough difference in animations, but not annoy the viewer with every possible animation available. Remember, less is always more.

Inset - Bottom Left

The "Inset - bottom left" animation adds a transition from Video 1 to Video 2 that replaces the scene from Video 1 by overwriting it with a growing rectangle that starts in the upper right-hand corner of Video 1 and expands in the direction of the lower left-hand corner of Video 1. The scene from Video 2 is visible in the growing rectangle.

Inset - Bottom Right

The "Inset - bottom right" animation adds a transition from Video 1 to Video 2 that replaces the scene from Video 1 by overwriting it with a growing rectangle that starts in the upper left-hand corner of Video 1 and expands in the direction of the lower right-hand corner of Video 1. The scene from Video 2 is visible in the growing rectangle.

Inset - Top Left

The "Inset - top left" animation adds a transition from Video 1 to Video 2 that replaces the scene from Video 1 by overwriting it with a growing rectangle that starts in the lower right-hand corner of Video 1 and expands in the direction of the upper left-hand corner of Video 1. The scene from Video 2 is visible in the growing rectangle.

Inset - Top Right

The "Inset - top right" animation adds a transition from Video 1 to Video 2 that replaces the scene from Video 1 by overwriting it with a growing rectangle that starts in the lower left-hand corner of Video 1 and expands in the direction of the upper right-hand corner of Video 1. The scene from Video 2 is visible in the growing rectangle.

Iris

The Iris animation adds a transition from Video 1 to Video 2 that replaces the scene from Video 1 by growing a plus-shaped block from the center of Video 1 outward. The scene from Video 2 is visible in the growing plus-shaped block.

Reveal Down

The "Reveal down" animation adds a transition from Video 1 to Video 2 that replaces the scene from Video 1 by moving a rectangle-shaped block from the top of the screen to the bottom. The scene from Video 2 is visible in the rectangle as it moves down.

Reveal Right

The "Reveal right" animation adds a transition from Video 1 to Video 2 that replaces the scene from Video 1 by moving a rectangle-shaped block from the left edge of Video 1 to the right edge. The scene from Video 2 is visible in the rectangle as it moves to the right.

Roll

The Roll animation adds a transition from Video 1 to Video 2 that replaces the scene from Video 1 by "rolling" the scene of Video 1 up and to the right of the screen. The effect is seen as if Video 2 is hidden under Video 1 and is exposed as Video 1 is pivoted from the lower left-hand corner of the screen, similar to a drawbridge opening.

Shrink In

The "Shrink in" animation adds a transition from Video 1 to Video 2 that replaces the scene from Video 1 by shrinking the scene of Video 1 from all edges until it finally disappears in the center of the screen. The scene from Video 2 is visible behind the shrinking Video 1.

Slide

The Slide animation adds a transition from Video 1 to Video 2 that replaces the scene from Video 1 by moving the entire Video 1 screen from the bottom of the screen to the top. The scene from Video 2 is visible as Video 1 is "pushed off" the screen.

Slide Up

The "Slide up" animation adds a transition from Video 1 to Video 2 that replaces the scene from Video 1 by moving the entire Video 1 screen from the bottom of the screen to the top and shrinking it at the same time. The scene from Video 2 is visible as Video 1 is "pushed off" the screen.

Spin

The Spin animation adds a transition from Video 1 to Video 2 that replaces the scene from Video 1 by shrinking and spinning the scene of Video 1 from all edges until it finally disappears in the center of the screen. The scene from Video 2 is visible behind the spinning and shrinking Video 1.

Split Horizontal

The "Split horizontal" animation adds a transition from Video 1 to Video 2 that replaces the scene from Video 1 by growing the entire Video 2 screen from the center of the screen to the top and bottom edges. The visual effect is as if Video 2 were growing toward the top and bottom of the screen.

Split Vertical

The "Split vertical" animation adds a transition from Video 1 to Video 2 that replaces the scene from Video 1 by growing the entire Video 2 screen from the center of the screen to the left and right edges. The visual effect is as if Video 2 were growing toward the right and left of the screen.

Shatters

The Shatters category offers a total of six different animations. The icon and name of each animation appear in Figure 5-11, along with a brief explanation of the animation's visual activity.

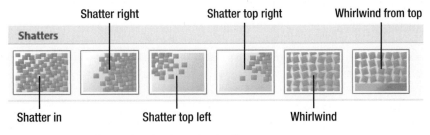

Figure 5-11. All six animation icons for the Shatters category.

Shatter In

The "Shatter in" animation adds a transition from Video 1 to Video 2 that appears as if the scene of Video 1 is shattered into small squares of glass that quickly fade away and reveal Video 2 beneath it.

Shatter Right

The "Shatter right" animation adds a transition from Video 1 to Video 2 that appears as if the scene of Video 1 is shattered into small squares of glass that quickly fade and move to the right side of the screen, revealing Video 2 beneath it.

Shatter Top-Left

The "Shatter top-left" animation adds a transition from Video 1 to Video 2 that appears as if the scene of Video 1 is shattered into small squares of glass that quickly fade and move to the upper left-hand corner of the screen, revealing Video 2 beneath it.

Shatter Top-Right

The "Shatter top-right" animation adds a transition from Video 1 to Video 2 that appears as if the scene of Video 1 is shattered into small squares of glass that quickly fade and move to the upper right-hand corner of the screen, revealing Video 2 beneath it.

Whirlwind

The Whirlwind animation adds a transition from Video 1 to Video 2 that appears as if the scene of Video 1 is spun away with small circle and square-shaped blocks evenly placed on the screen. The small blocks spin and fade, revealing Video 2 underneath.

Whirlwind from Top

The Whirlwind animation adds a transition from Video 1 to Video 2 that appears as if the scene of Video 1 is spun away with small circle- and square-shaped blocks that drop from the top of the screen toward the bottom. The small blocks fall, spin and fade, revealing Video 2 underneath.

Sweeps & Curls

The "Sweeps & curls" category offers a total of ten different animations. The icon and name of each animation appear in Figure 5-12 along with a brief explanation of the animation's visual activity.

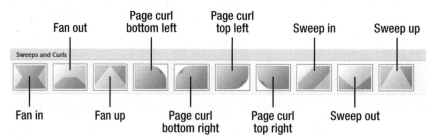

Figure 5-12. All ten animation icons for the Sweeps & Curls category.

Fan In

The "Fan in" animation adds a transition from Video 1 to Video 2 that appears as if the scene of Video 1 is being swept from the outer edges of the screen to the center, revealing Video 2 beneath it.

Fan Out

The "Fan out" animation adds a transition from Video 1 to Video 2 that appears as if the scene of Video 1 is being swept in a circular motion starting at the center of the screen and ending up fading out in the center of the screen, revealing Video 2 beneath it.

Fan Up

The "Fan up" animation adds a transition from Video 1 to Video 2 that appears as if the scene of Video 1 is being swept from the bottom of the screen to the left and right top edges of the screen, revealing Video 2 beneath it.

Page Curl Bottom Left

The "Page curl bottom left" animation adds a transition from Video 1 to Video 2 that appears as if the scene of Video 1 is a page of a book being turned; the direction of the turn is from the upper right-hand corner to the bottom left, revealing Video 2 beneath it.

Page Curl Bottom Right

The "Page curl bottom right" animation adds a transition from Video 1 to Video 2 that appears as if the scene of Video 1 is a page of a book being turned; the direction of the turn is from the upper left-hand corner to the bottom right, revealing Video 2 beneath it.

Page Curl Top Left

The "Page curl top left" animation adds a transition from Video 1 to Video 2 that appears as if the scene of Video 1 is a page of a book being turned; the direction of the turn is from the bottom right-hand corner to the top left, revealing Video 2 beneath it.

Page Curl Top Right

The "Page curl top right" animation adds a transition from Video 1 to Video 2 that appears as if the scene of Video 1 is a page of a book being turned; the direction of the turn is from the bottom left-hand corner to the top right, revealing Video 2 beneath it.

Sweep In

The "Sweep in" animation adds a transition from Video 1 to Video 2 that appears as if the left and right edges of Video 1 are being swept to the center of the screen until it fades away, revealing Video 2 beneath it.

Sweep Out

The "Sweep out" animation adds a transition from Video 1 to Video 2 that appears as if the top left and top right edges of Video 1 are being swept down and away from the center of the screen, revealing Video 2 beneath it.

Sweep Up

The "Sweep up" animation adds a transition from Video 1 to Video 2 that appears as if the bottom left and bottom right edges of Video 1 are being swept up and away from the center of the screen, revealing Video 2 beneath it.

Wipes

The Wipes category offers a total of eight different animations. The icon and name of each animation appear in Figure 5-13, along with a brief explanation of the animation's visual activity.

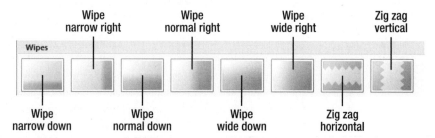

Figure 5-13. All eight animation icons for the Wipes category.

Wipe Narrow Down

The "Wipe narrow down" animation adds a transition from Video 1 to Video 2 that appears as if Video 1 is being "wiped" away from top to bottom, revealing Video 2 beneath it. The wipe effect is represented by a thin bar moving from the top of the screen to the bottom.

Wipe Narrow Right

The "Wipe narrow right" animation adds a transition from Video 1 to Video 2 that appears as if Video 1 is being "wiped" away from left to right, revealing Video 2 beneath it. The wipe effect is represented by a thin bar moving from the left of the screen to the right.

Wipe Normal Down

The "Wipe narrow down" animation adds a transition from Video 1 to Video 2 that appears as if Video 1 is being "wiped" away from top to bottom, revealing Video 2 beneath it. The wipe effect is represented by a bar moving from the top of the screen to the bottom.

Wipe Normal Right

The "Wipe normal right" animation adds a transition from Video 1 to Video 2 that appears as if Video 1 is being "wiped" away from left to right, revealing Video 2 beneath it. The wipe effect is represented by a bar moving from the left of the screen to the right.

Wipe Wide Down

The "Wipe wide down" animation adds a transition from Video 1 to Video 2 that appears as if Video 1 is being "wiped" away from top to bottom, revealing Video 2 beneath it. The wipe effect is represented by a thick bar moving from the top of the screen to the bottom.

Wipe Wide Right

The "Wipe wide right" animation adds a transition from Video 1 to Video 2 that appears as if Video 1 is being "wiped" away from left to right, revealing Video 2 beneath it. The wipe effect is represented by a thick bar moving from the left of the screen to the right.

Zig Zag Horizontal

The "Zig zag horizontal" animation adds a transition from Video 1 to Video 2 that appears as if Video 1 is being "wiped" away by zig zag lines, revealing Video 2 beneath it. The effect is represented by two zig zag lines, one moving from the center of the screen to the top and the other moving from the center of the screen to the bottom.

Zig Zag Vertical

The "Zig zag vertical" animation adds a transition from Video 1 to Video 2 that appears as if Video 1 is being "wiped" away by zig zag lines, revealing Video 2 beneath it. The effect is represented by two zig zag lines, one moving from the center of the screen to the left side and the other moving from the center of the screen to the right side.

Animation Speed

Now that you know about the different categories of animations available to you, I'd like to also explain that you can control the speed at which the animation runs.

Take a look at Figure 5-14 and you'll notice that, after selecting an animation, you also gain control of the Duration of the animation.

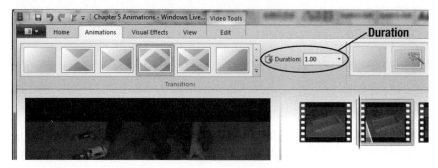

Figure 5-14. You can control the duration of any animation.

By default, all animations are set to run for one second. You can change this value by clicking the small arrow and picking a time from the drop-down menu that appears. Your choices run from between .25 seconds to 2 seconds, but you can type in a different value for the Duration if you like as shown in Figure 5-15.

Figure 5-15. Increase or decrease the duration of an animation.

If you wish to use a different value for the time, you must type the value into the box. In Figure 5-15, I've configured this animation to run for a full five seconds. The effect is that the animation runs slower. You'll want to experiment with the value for Duration based on the length of the two videos that it separates. For short videos, a long animation can actually be disruptive to the screen; consider shortening the animation by reducing its duration to .25 or .5 seconds.

Adding Animations to Photos

Just like videos, any photographs that you import into your Library can also have animations that provide a transition. Figure 5-16 shows that I've imported a few photographs from the workbench assembly. I've placed them between my videos.

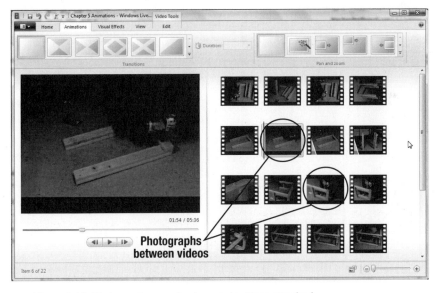

Figure 5-16. Photographs can also have animations attached.

ExplainED

Remember that videos in the library have the dotted "film" edges to indicate they are videos, versus photographs, which have plain edges.

Click a photograph that you've added to your Library and switch to the *Animations* tab. You'll notice that a new set of animations are available to you along the right side of the Animation tab as indicated in Figure 5-17.

For photographs, you can always add one of the regular animations covered earlier in this chapter. A Wipe animation added to a photograph inserted after a video, for example, would show the video playing, followed by a wipe and a five-second display of the photograph.

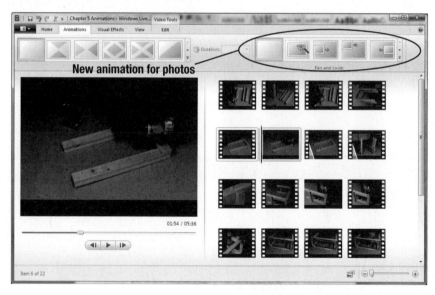

Figure 5-17. New animations are available for photographs.

The new animations available for photographs aren't so much animations as they are movements of your photographs on the screen. Because a photo is static, one way to add a little bang to your photographs is to move them around the screen. This may be a bit difficult to visualize and it's impossible to demonstrate with words, so once again I encourage you to just apply them to photographs in your Library and see what they do.

ExplainED

The default time that a photograph will display is five seconds. To change this, click the photograph, select the Edit tab, and change the Duration time to the desired running time for the photograph. Remember, with most animations being one second in length, the full viewing time of the photo will be reduced to four seconds. Increase the length of your photos to give your viewers enough time to properly view (and appreciate) your photographs.

To view all the new photograph animations available, click the More button, as shown in Figure 5-18.

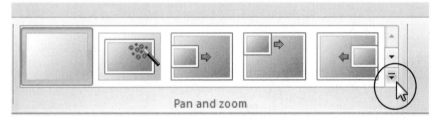

Figure 5-18. The More button gives you access to new animations.

After clicking the More button, a drop-down menu will appear with all the new animations available. Figure 5-19 shows all the animations; you can view them all like this by clicking and dragging the expand bar down.

Figure 5-19 shows 18 different animation icons available, plus one called Automatic and another called None. The None selection will remove any animation you've added to a photograph. The Automatic animation will randomly select one of the other 18 animations and apply it.

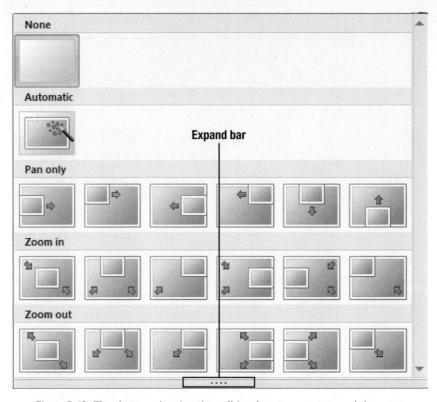

Figure 5-19. The photograph animations all involve movement around the screen.

The effect of each animation is shown by its icon. The arrows point to the starting point of the photograph, and the smaller box shows its final stopping point. Note that the photo never changes, but instead the animation is used to move the full image around the screen. It gives the effect of movement, but the photo, being static, stays the same. The photo, instead, is enlarged so it's bigger than the screen and can be moved around without a black border being visible around it.

For example, Figure 5-20 shows that I've selected a Zoom out animation. The photograph is displayed full size to the left of the Library. The animation icon's arrows tell me the photograph will start full size and shrink (from the upper left and bottom right-hand corners) and self-center on the screen.

Figure 5-20. One of the Zoom out animations applied to a photo.

Figure 5-21 shows the final photograph after the animation has completed.

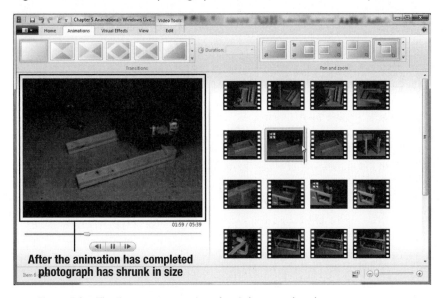

Figure 5-21. The Zoom out animation after it has completed.

Animation Overload

It is fully possible to overuse animations. As you experiment with the various animations, you're likely to find some that visually conflict. By this, I mean that some animations just don't seem to work well together, and can irritate the viewer (consciously or subconsciously) by taking away his or her focus from the scene at hand and making the animation the subject of attention.

The best animations are subtle and fast, but also useful. When transitioning between two short videos, ask yourself if an animation is truly necessary. If the two videos are simply different views of the same place, object, or person, an animation will most likely not be necessary. Animations are useful when the scenes change from one subject to another, such as when the scenes change from an outside shot of a sunset to an inside shot of a family dinner, or from a child blowing out a birthday cake to a scene of the child opening presents.

Combining animations with music, voice-overs, and good editing is a skill. Fortunately, your skills will improve as you work more videos; your editing will get better (and faster), your use of sound will be more relevant and on cue, and your animations will provide fluid transitions that the viewers hardly notices because they are so caught up in the scenes, music, and narrative.

Remember, less is more. So with animations, use them sparingly and always experiment with more than one to find the right speed and movement that makes the transition an easy one on the eyes.

What's Next?

Chapter 6 is a short one, but it's one of those chapters that allow you to add some fun and twisty modifications to your movies using visual effects. Not all of your movies will use visual effects, but when you're looking for more visual impact than animations provide to you, you'll find that the visual effects offered by Movie Maker deliver.

Chapter 6

Playing with Visual Effects

Not every movie you'll be editing and sharing with others needs to be so serious. You might find yourself putting together a nice music video of your latest snowboarding venture, or maybe a video for a friend of her latest art show gathering. There are plenty of times where a movie could use a little extra whiz-bang special effects and editing. And when that time comes, you'll want to take a look at the visual effects that Movie Maker brings to the table.

Visual effects differ from Animations (see Chapter 5). Animations don't alter the actual video, but provide transitions from one scene to the next. (Movie Maker should really have renamed Animations to Transitions, and then it wouldn't be so confusing.) Visual effects actually make visual changes to your videos: changing a color scene to black and white, for instance, or giving a scene a ripple effect or flipping it so it's a mirrored image of the original.

As with Animations, however, you can overdo it with visual effects. Too many of these special effects can often irritate viewers and distract them from the main focus of the scene. Visual effects are meant to be fun, creative ways to give a scene some extra punch, but not every scene needs it.

I'm going to go over all the various types of visual effects that Movie Maker offers; hopefully you'll find a few that are interesting enough to include in your next movie.

Types of Visual Effects

Take a look at Figure 6-1. I'm continuing with the individual videos of my workbench assembly. Animations have been added between some of the videos. (See Chapter 5 for more information on animations.)

Figure 6-1. My videos with Animations between some of them.

ExplainED

With this particular movie, I'm not really interested in adding visual effects. This is a tutorial video showing me assembling a workbench. I want the focus of each scene to be the work I'm doing, and I don't want to distract my viewer with any odd coloring changes or strange distortions of the screen.

Although I'm not going to be adding any visual effects to my final movie, I'm going to use these videos to demonstrate to you the various visual effects found in Movie Maker. The only difference is that when I'm done with adding the visual effects, I'm not going to save my work; I don't wish to keep them.

To work with visual effects, you'll start by clicking the Visual Effects tab, as shown in Figure 6-2.

Figure 6-2. The Visual Effects tab has some fun and unusual video effects.

Learning about visual effects will be much easier if you're actually using them, so follow along with me by opening Movie Maker and importing a few videos. Click the *Visual Effects* tab, and then click the *More* button, as indicated in Figure 6-3.

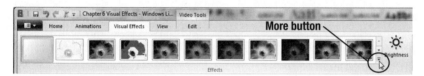

Figure 6-3. The More button gives you access to all of the visual effects.

Clicking the *More* button reveals a drop-down menu like the one seen in Figure 6-4.

Figure 6-4. Visual effects are broken into five categories.

117

Scroll down this menu and you'll see a total of five categories: No Effect, Artistic, Black & White, Mirror, and Motions & Fades. Each category (with the exception of No Effect) has a collection of icons that represent a different type of visual effect.

ExplainED

To view all of the visual effects at once (instead of using the scroll bar), click and hold the bottom edge of the drop-down menu and drag it down until it expands, as shown in Figure 6-4.

Just like animations (see chapter 5), you simply select a video in your Library, click the *Visual Effects* tab's *More* button, scroll through the categories, and pick a visual effect you want to apply. Moving your mouse pointer over a visual effect provides a 2-3 second preview in the Editing screen, as shown in Figure 6-5.

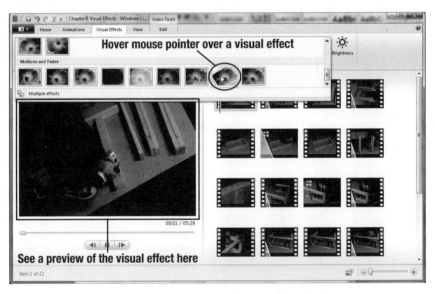

Figure 6-5. Hover your mouse over a visual effect to see a preview.

Unlike animations, a visual effect is added only to the selected video. With animations, the transition is applied between two videos. If you wish to have a visual effect applied to two movies that play back to back, you'll need to select each video individually and apply the same effect.

Once you've applied a visual effect, a small icon (it looks like a small four-pane window) is added to the upper left-hand corner of the video as seen in Figure 6-6.

Figure 6-6. A small icon is added to let you know a visual effect has been added.

To remove a visual effect, click a video with a visual effect icon and select the No Effect option from the More button's drop-down menu (refer to Figure 6-4).

There aren't as many visual effects options in Movie Maker as there are animations options, but I'd still like to go over each one and give a short, non-technical explanation of what each does to a video. There are some visual effects that I will likely never use, but I can't say that for your videos.

NotED

Unlike animations, the very first video in your Library can have any visual effect added to it. While I typically avoid adding effects to my more serious movies, a visual effect can make for a nice opening scene. Consider creating a small montage of scenes from all the videos in your movie and using them (along with text, covered in Chapter 7) with an applied visual effect to create an eye-catching movie opener.

Artistic

The Artistic category offers three different visual effects. The icon and name of each effect appear in Figure 6-7, along with a brief explanation of the visual effect.

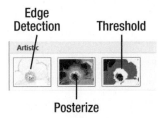

Figure 6-7. All three effects icons for the Artistic category.

NotED

These effects are definitely unusual and should be used with care; all three add some extreme distortion to the selected video. Possible uses for these effects include opening credits and closing credits, where the viewer does not necessarily need to see a lot of detail in the video(s) being played.

Edge Detection

Edge Detection converts a video into a "blueprint"-like image. A white background appears, and any objects or persons in the video are given a sharp outline that does a fairly decent job of keeping the focus of the video intact.

Edge Detection is a perfect effect for a technical video. Consider using it in the intro and applying it to a picture of the item (software, product, what have you) that is the subject of your video. The blueprint-like effect should be easily recognizable.

Posterize

The Posterize effect applies a medium-level of distortion to any video. It can make a dark scene almost impossible to discern. It applies a certain level of "static" to a screen, giving objects and persons a fuzzy, pixel-ish glow.

Use this effect sparingly, as it distorts the video enough to make details difficult to see. Possible uses include ending credits, where you can apply lighter text to the darker background or maybe use it with small animated transitions between videos, where you wish the viewer to focus on text applied over the background video.

Threshold

The Threshold effect adds the highest level of distortion to a video. Dark areas of the video are converted to black, and everything else is given a colorful and pixel-ish glow.

I'm not a fan of this effect, because of the amount of distortion it applies. However, I could easily see it being used for artistic videos in which each video closes with the last 5 or 10 seconds having the Threshold effect added as a visual clue that one scene is ending and another beginning.

Black & White

The Black & White category offers a total of six different effects. The icon and name of each effect appear in Figure 6-8, along with a brief explanation of the visual effect.

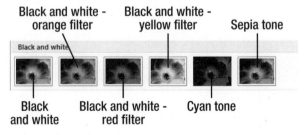

Figure 6-8. All six effect icons for the Black & White category.

Black and White

This one is easy. Your full-color video is converted into a black and white video. It is a very nice visual effect that doesn't really take away from the subject of the video.

Black and White is useful for opening scenes where you wish the viewer to focus on text or possibly a voice-over. Then, when the moment is right, change your movie over to full color for a dramatic effect.

Black and White - Orange Filter, Red Filter, Yellow Filter

These three effects convert color videos into black and white, but also apply a filter that, in theory, is supposed to tone down certain colors and make others more noticeable. To be honest, I could not detect much of a difference between the three filters, but you may have a video that was shot outdoors or in certain lighting that might be improved by adding a filter.

Filters should be used carefully, because viewers are typically able to discern something unusual from a scene where the natural colors have been changed. The use of filters is sometimes viewed as a mistake or a glitch in a video rather than the intended effect, so use it only where it will be extremely obvious that you've tampered with the original video.

Cyan Tone

The Cyan Tone applies a bluish filter over your video, making it appear darker. This effect might be useful with a video that is too bright, but the bluish tint that is applied is not very pleasing to the eye, in my opinion.

Sepia Tone

The Sepia Tone, like the Black and White effect, is a nice, visually pleasing effect that gives a video an antiquated look: colors are muted, and have a brown/yellow coloring effect instead of the grey provided by the Black and White effect.

One interesting usage for it is to apply it to the opening credits where a video is playing behind the text; the antique look can be used for wedding videos or older family videos, and gives a hint to viewers that older movies are likely to be shared.

Mirror

The Mirror category offers only two different effects. The icon and name of each effect appear in Figure 6-9, along with a brief explanation of the visual effect.

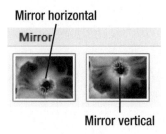

Figure 6-9. Two effects are available for the Mirror category.

Mirror Horizontal

By selecting this effect, the video is flipped on the horizontal axis. Anything in your video that appears on the left side of the screen now appears on the right side. This effect can be used in a fun way by splitting a video into two equal halves and flipping it halfway through using the mirror horizontal effect. It grabs the viewer's attention, but doesn't really take attention away from the action on the screen.

Mirror Vertical

Using this effect, the video is flipped on the vertical axis. Anything appearing at the top of your video is now displayed at the bottom. This is another fun effect, but it can be distracting to your viewer if the action on screen is too complex.

The Mirror effects are fun, but don't overuse them. Possible uses are for videos where fast-paced music has been added to enhance action scenes. Use the mirror to give a video a slight visual "kick" without changing anything other than the orientation. The viewer will understand they are looking at a mirror image from the animation. It's not useful, however, when text is visible on the screen. Backwards text, even in the background, is an annoyance to any viewer.

Motions & Fades

The Motions & Fades category offers a total of nine different effects. The icon and name of each effect appear in Figure 6-10, along with a brief explanation of the visual effect.

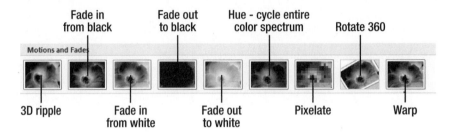

Figure 6-10. All nine effect icons for the Motions & Fades category.

3D Ripple

This is a nice effect for an opening or closing scene, but don't use it too much. It a nice water ripple effect that continues through the entire video, so it can get annoying if used too long. It's useful for opening credits or transitions between individual videos where text may be applied. Try it out and you'll see how great text looks.

Fade In from Black

This is a nice visual effect that can be used often with little irritation to your viewer. It simply starts from a completely black screen and then your video fades in and begins playing. It's considered "old school," but it's definitely an effect that works well and doesn't overwhelm your viewers.

Fade In from White

Just like the Fade in from Black effect, this effect starts instead with a completely white screen before having your video fade in. Again, this is one of the few effects that can be used often and doesn't overwhelm a viewer.

Fade Out to Black

This effect allows the selected video to play through its entirety and then fades out to a completely black screen. This is a nice effect to use when closing a movie out and moving to closing credits. It's also a useful effect for using within a movie when changing to a new video with a new location or a different subject.

Fade Out to White

This effect allows the selected video to play through its entirety and then fades out to a completely white screen. This is a nice effect to use when opening a movie with opening credits or a title screen. It's also a useful effect for using within a movie when changing to a new video with a new location or a different subject.

Most viewers are able to understand that the Fade Out effects typically signal a change of scene. Don't use them in between videos shot in the same location; they are best used when the time/day, place, or subject of the next video has changed.

Hue – Cycle Entire Color Spectrum

This effect isn't as annoying as it sounds, but you should use it sparingly. It changes the color of the screen by applying a red, purple, blue, and other filters, one at a time. This is another effect that could be used with opening or closing credits. It's too odd of an effect to put into your normal videos where you wish the reader to focus on details.

Pixelate

This is similar to the Animation transition of the same name. The effect starts with your video in an un-altered format, but quickly distorts the screen. Small squares (pixels) quickly change to large squares, causing whatever is on the screen to become non-discernible when the video ends. This effect could be useful for closing out a movie and moving into closing credits. And since it looks a little "techy," it can be interesting to use in videos where the subject is technical in nature.

Rotate 360

This effect can be useful in an opening credit scene. Because the video will be rotating counter-clockwise, it is difficult for the viewer to pay attention to whatever is being displayed in the video. It's more useful as an eye-catching effect to get the viewer's attention before starting the actual movie.

Warp

Like the 3D Ripple effect, the Warp effect distorts the video by twisting the screen along the horizontal axis. It's not as annoying as it sounds, but viewers are not likely to want to watch it for long stretches or for videos where attention to detail is required. This is another effect that is best used with a title or closing credit scene; it doesn't apply the effect to text, so don't use it with a video image that contains a lot of action that will take the viewer's attention away from the credits.

Using Effects

Using visual effects properly takes some practice. At first, you're likely to want to throw in all sorts of eye-catching effects, adding one to each individual video in your movie.

It's not uncommon to watch a movie made with Movie Maker and see scene-after-scene with visual effects thrown into the mix. It may look and sound fun to you, but put yourself in the position of a viewer of your movie and ask yourself some questions:

- Does an effect distract from the focus of a video?
- Does an effect make it hard to see details in a video?
- Does an effect darken or lighten the video too much?
- Are effects being displayed too quickly?
- Do the effects work well together or are the visuals too jarring?

Visual effects can make a video more fun and much more eye-catching, but your viewers are most likely watching your video for the content, not the special effects. Don't overwhelm your museum tour or baby's first steps with flips and warps and odd color changes.

Instead, save your special effects for those times when your viewer is likely to want their attention grabbed: Opening Title, change of direction in your movie, subtitles, and Closing Credits. (I'll cover adding titles, credits, and subtitles in Chapter 7.)

Brightness

One last item I want to share with you in this chapter is using the *Brightness* control on the *Visual Effects* tab, as indicated in Figure 6-11.

Figure 6-11. The Brightness control is located on the Visual Effects tab.

You can use the *Brightness* control with or without a Visual Effect. Simply click a video that you wish to lighten or darken and then click the Brightness control. A slider control will appear, as shown in Figure 6-12.

Figure 6-12. Brightness is controlled with a slider bar.

ExplainED

Not everyone buys and uses an external light source with their video recorders. This means that videos are often recorded in less than optimal lighting. Movie Maker's Brightness control can overcome this a bit, but don't rely on it too much. Artificially brightening a video can have the reverse effect of washing out brighter colors on the screen; a subject's white shirt will start to look like it glows if you apply too much brightening. If you tend to shoot videos in low lighting (indoor weddings, museums, and the like), consider purchasing an add-on light made for video cameras (check with the manufacturers to find a compatible lighting option).

Drag the bar to the left to darken the video, and drag the bar to the right to lighten the video. You may need to experiment and play your video completely through to determine the best setting for your brightness modification.

What's Next?

Coming up next in Chapter 7, I'm going to show you how to use text and color to make your videos more useful and fun. Text isn't just for an Opening Title and Closing Credits, however. Text can be used to help prepare your viewer for what's to come as well as for adding information that can't easily be provided by video (think dates or prices of items). Text is the final bit of editing you'll add to your movies before using Movie Maker to save, publish, and share your movies.

Chapter 7

Working with Text

Movie Maker can make your movies shine with its easy-to-use editing features and a bundle of special effects. With the right amount of cropping, clipping, ordering, and animations, you can put together a very entertaining and engaging movie that your viewers will enjoy watching.

But if your movies consist of nothing but sound and imagery, you're leaving out a key component that gives a movie a polished and finished touch: text.

You'll see text primarily used for opening titles and closing credits in most movies. And there's nothing wrong with using text for those elements. But if you're limiting your usage of text to only those two positions, start and end, you're really missing out on a useful tool that can make your movies shine.

In this chapter, I'm going to demonstrate how easy it is to add opening and closing credits, but also how to add text to any scene in any video. Text can be used for so many more things than titles and credits, and by the time you finish this chapter, you should have a better idea of where, how, and why to use text to make your movies even better.

Uses of Text

For this chapter, I'm going to cover four different uses of text and show you how to implement them in your own movies. These four types are:

- Opening title: You've seen this in every Hollywood movie you've ever seen: a big title giving the name of the movie. A title screen not only helps your viewer decide whether to keep watching ("Is this something I'm interested in?"), but it also provides him or her with a quick synopsis of the movie's subject ("Hey, this isn't our *Our Trip to Peru* movie!")

- Closing credits: Closing credits give you the ability to list not only those responsible for helping you with your movie (you don't have to list me in every one of your movies, just the first one), but also a chance to thank individuals and organizations, list special hardware used, and more.

- In-video callouts: You may find yourself putting a video into your movie that really needs some explanation, or maybe the viewer's attention needs to be focused on something specific in the scene. In-video callouts are bits of text embedded into an actual scene that help the viewer ("Watch the little boy in the shallow end of the pool!") Used correctly, they can be used to prep your viewer for something that happens quickly or needs to be labeled.

- Transition narration: Transition narrations are like opening titles and closing credits. They are simple screens that are embedded into your movie between certain scenes. They are useful for scene and date changes ("Nov 21 2009: Day 1 in Machu Picchu") or to just give your viewer more information to help him or her understand the scene to come.

These are by no means the only uses of text, but they'll get you started. There are no real rules for using text other than our old favorite: less is more. Use text when necessary, but try to keep it under control and allow the images in your movie to do the real work.

Opening Title

Take a look at Figure 7-1. It's nothing fancy, just an opening title for my new movie.

As you can see, my title is white text on a black background. It runs for five seconds and then the first video begins to play. I'd like to make it a little more eye-catching, so I'm going to start over and show you how to add a title and modify it a bit.

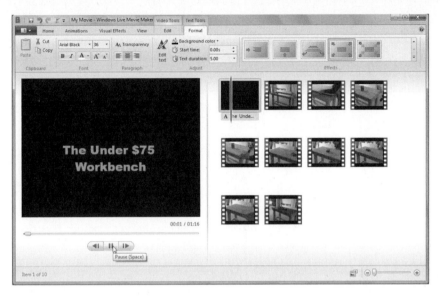

Figure 7-1. A simple title for my new movie.

To add a title screen, click the first video in your Library, as shown in Figure 7-2.

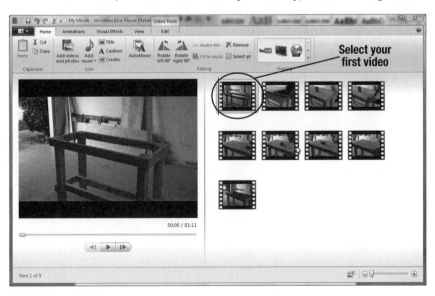

Figure 7-2. Select your first video to add an opening title screen.

Next, select the *Home* tab and click the *Title* button, as shown in Figure 7-3.

Figure 7-3. The Title button on the Home tab.

A new five-second video is added at the beginning of your Library. (Yes, it's a video; it can be trimmed and a few animations and visual effects can be added to it, but let's first look at a few text basics.) Click the title screen video and you'll see that, right now, it's nothing more than some placeholder text on a black background. See Figure 7-4.

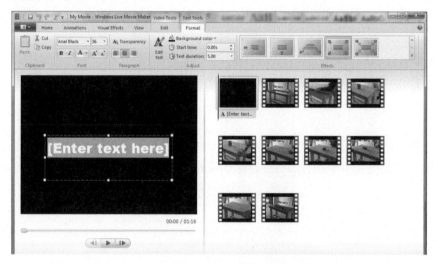

Figure 7-4. An opening title screen is added with placeholder text.

Go ahead and type in your movie's title. You can use the small white boxes surrounding the text to enlarge or shrink the text space. Left click any part of the dotted line while holding down the mouse button and you can drag the text around the small screen; release the mouse when you're satisfied with the text placement, as in Figure 7-5.

NotED

Note that when the title screen is added, a new tab called Format appears on the toolbar along the top of the screen. I'll go over this tab's features shortly, but it will only be visible when you are working with text. If you click any video in your Library that does not have text added to it, this tab will disappear.

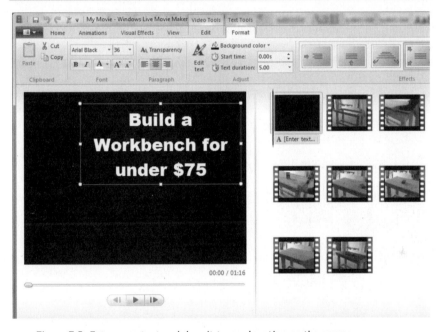

Figure 7-5. Enter your text and drag it to any location on the screen.

ExplainED

The default font used for text is Arial Black and the font size is 36. You're not limited to this font and font size, however. The same goes for the background color. Movie Maker starts with these defaults, but gives you the ability to modify it.

That may be all you want to do, but let me show you how to modify the title a bit. I'll start with the font and font size. I first select the text with my mouse. Next, I click the Format tab and use the drop-down font and font size menus shown in Figure 7-6 to find a font and size that I like.

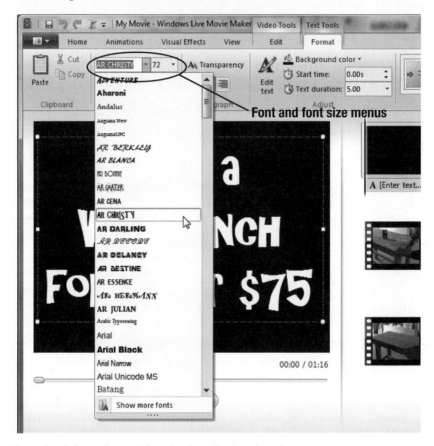

Figure 7-6. Select a font and font size from the two drop-down menus.

NotED

The fonts listed in Figure 7-6 are the fonts I have installed on my computer. Your list will most likely look different and will display only those fonts that are installed on your system.

Next, I'd like to change the background color. This is done by clicking the "Background color" button shown in Figure 7-7. Select a color from the ones shown, and the black background changes to your new selection.

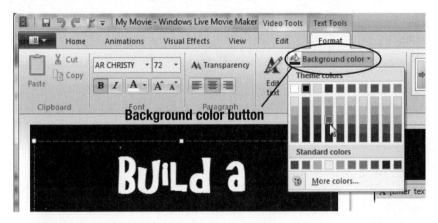

Figure 7-7. Select a new background color from the pop-up box.

NotED

If you'd like to use a color that's not displayed in the pop-up selection box in Figure 7-7, then click the "More colors" option at the bottom of the pop-up box and then click the Define Custom Colors option to mix a custom color.

The text is still white, but I can easily change that by selecting the text and then clicking the Text Color button, as shown in Figure 7-8.

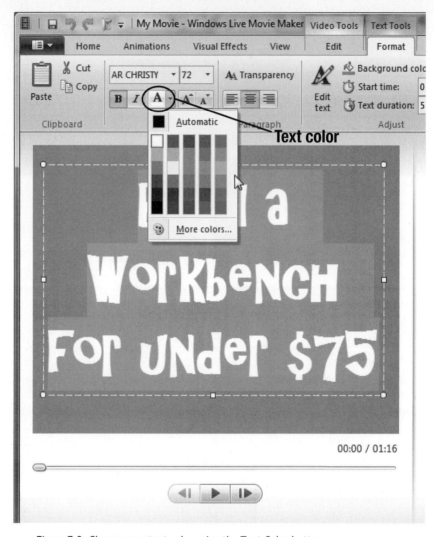

Figure 7-8. Change your text color using the Text Color button.

Figure 7-9 shows my new title screen, complete with new font, enlarged font size, and new colors for both font and background.

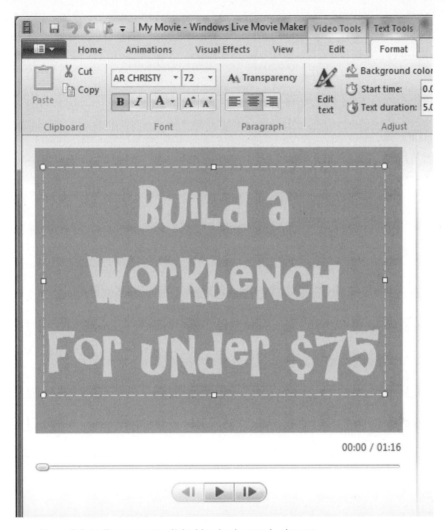

Figure 7-9. Yellow text on a light blue background — honest.

Before I leave the title screen section, I want to cover just a few more things you can do to add some pop to your opening credits.

Formatting

On the Format tab, there are additional options to format your text with bold and italics; you can also right-, left-, or center-justify the text. (I'll cover the Transparency button in the "In-Video Callout" section later in this chapter.)

Running Time

Your opening title is given a five-second run-time by default. You can increase or decrease this by staying in the Format tab and entering a new value (in seconds) in the Text Duration box. Don't make the duration of your opening title too short, or your viewers might not have time to read it!

Animations

As with videos, your opening title screen can use a limited number of animations from the *Animations* tab (see Chapter 5). But the *Format* tab also provides you with some very fun effects that are just for text — Figure 7-10 shows these. I've selected the spinning text effect so the title whirls on the screen for a split second before displaying properly. Just click the *Effects* drop-down menu and browse through the effects until you find one you like.

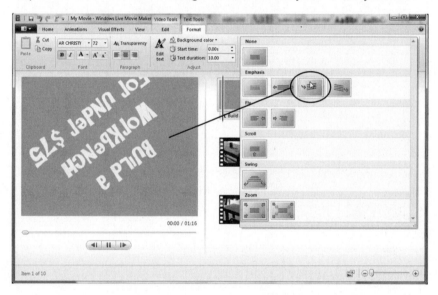

Figure 7-10. Text Effects can add a nice special effect to your title screen.

Closing Credits

Closing credits are created and modified just like the opening title screen. To add closing credits, click the *Credits* button shown in Figure 7-11. (Unlike selecting the first video to create an opening title, you don't have to select the last video in the Library to add credits. Movie Maker is smart enough to add the credits video to the end of the Library.)

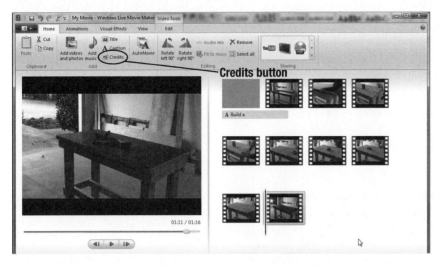

Figure 7-11. Credits are added after the last video in your Library.

A familiar-looking screen appears with white text on a black background, as shown in Figure 7-12.

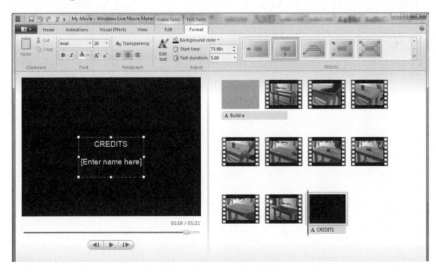

Figure 7-12. Credits start as white text on a black background.

You change the text, font color, size, and background color using the *Format* tab just like you did with the title screen. But there's a slight problem here: you only have the one screen for your credits. What if you want to have credits similar to movies, with scrolling text or text that disappears and is replaced by more text?

That's easy enough. Simply treat each of your closing credit screens as an individual five-second video. This means adding another credit video to the end by clicking the Credits button again. As seen in Figure 7-13, another five-second credits video is added to the end.

Figure 7-13. The next credits screen is simply another short video.

AdvancED

You can add more opening credits if you like, too. Instead of a single opening title, if you'd like to have more text displayed (maybe an actors list: James Floyd Kelly as The Mad Scientist), simply click the existing opening title in the Library and click the Title button again. A new five-second video is added. Shift them around as you see fit.

Try to keep your closing credits consistent by keeping the font, font size, font color, and background color the same from credit video to credit video.

And, just like title videos, you can add a few special effects to your closing credits by selecting them from the Effects drop-down menu.

ExplainED

For scrolling credits (that roll from bottom to top, just like in a Hollywood movie), select the Scroll effect for every closing credit video. When played, the text will scroll up, with each closing credit's text rolling upward one after another.

In-Video Callouts

Take a look at Figure 7-14. It shows a scene from a video where I'm drilling a 1/8-inch pilot hole for a wood screw. The pilot hole isn't required, but it does make it easier to screw the larger diameter screw into the wood. But from the video, the viewer cannot determine what size drill bit I'm using to drill that pilot hole.

Figure 7-14. What size drill bit is he using?

Now take a look at Figure 7-15. It lets the viewer know that I'm drilling a pilot hole with a 1/8-inch drill bit.

Figure 7-15. In-video callouts can help explain a scene or point out details.

In-video callouts are simply text that you can place anywhere in your video. I use them to provide little details about what the viewer is watching, but you can easily use them to add dates and times to scenes, explain steps ("Step 1: Drill the table top"), or even add lyrics to a song that's playing onscreen.

ExplainED

Of course, you want to format them with the right size, font, and color so they stand out in the scene. I had originally picked a red font color, but it was too distracting and bright; yellow was too dim and blended with the scene. I settled on blue and gave it a spin effect (yes, you can use effects), which draws the viewer's attention momentarily.

Adding in-video callouts is extremely simple. Select the video that you wish to add a callout to and then click the *Caption* button shown in Figure 7-16.

Figure 7-16. In-video callouts are added with the Caption button.

After clicking the *Caption* button, a new text box appears on the scene, as shown in Figure 7-17.

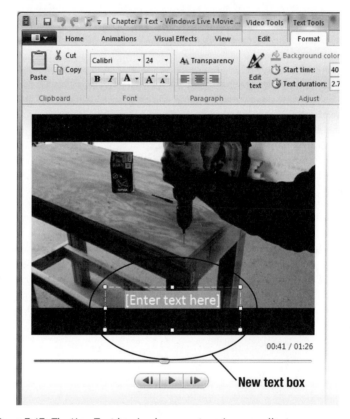

Figure 7-17. The New Text box is where you type in your callout.

You can drag the text box anywhere onscreen by left-clicking and holding any portion of the dotted line making up the box. Clicking any of the small white boxes will allow you to resize the text box.

NotED

Notice in Figure 7-17 that the text box is at the bottom of the screen. You can use this location (and a smaller font size) to easily add subtitles to your movies. Subtitles are not only useful for the hearing impaired, but they can also be helpful when music or background noises make it difficult to hear someone speaking.

Use the standard *Format* tab editing buttons to change the font, font size, and color; and feel free to change the duration of the text, its starting point in the video, and add an effect if you like.

ExplainED

Your movie will have a much more polished look to it if you keep the font and font size consistent throughout your movie for all callouts. The callout color should be kept the same if possible, but due to the color of the background scene, you may have to change it occasionally to make it easier to read. Try to stick with two or three colors instead of using every color of the rainbow.

Figure 7-18 shows my new callout that explains that I'm using 2-inch wood screws for attaching the worktable's top.

While I'm showing you how to add text to an actual scene in your movie, this is a good time to demonstrate the use of the Transparency button on the Format tab shown in Figure 7-19. At this point in the scene, I've added a large warning bit of text that runs for the first five seconds of the video (the default time for any text you add using the *Caption* button).

Figure 7-18. Another callout with a slightly different color.

ExplainED

You can always increase the running time of your in-video callout by selecting the text, and changing the value in the Duration box on the Format tab. (Modifying running times can also be done on the Edit tab.)

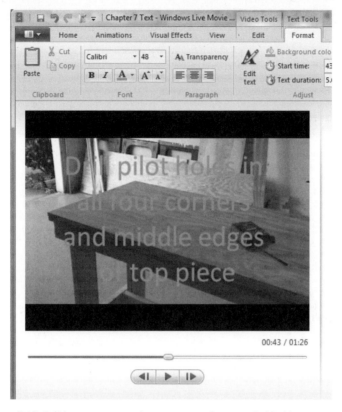

Figure 7-19. Solid text can sometimes cover up the scene behind it.

The text is bright and solid, but there's a problem. A few seconds into the video, I'm pointing out a few areas on the tabletop that are partially obscured by the text. What I need to do is make the text a little more transparent so it doesn't obscure the action behind it.

To fix this, I select the text, click the *Transparency* button, and use the slider bar that appears in Figure 7-20. Dragging the bar to the right increases the transparency.

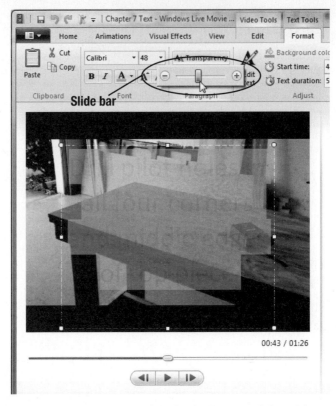

Figure 7-20. Use the Transparency slider bar by dragging it left or right.

After experimenting with the transparency of the text and playing the video to see the results, Figure 7-21 shows the scene with the text at about 50% transparency, and the action in the scene more visible now. The text is readable and the viewer can see where I'm pointing a bit better.

Figure 7-21. Transparent text is less distracting but still readable.

Transition Narration

The last usage of text that I want to cover is transition narration. In Chapter 5 I covered transitions that provide a brief animation between videos and changes in scene. But transition narration uses text instead of visual effects that blend one video into the next.

Take a look at Figure 7-22. I've added a transition narration between the second and third videos in the Library.

Figure 7-22. A transition narration using text.

Just like any other text element in your movie, you can change the font, font size, and font color and have access to all the other *Format* tab features. You can change the running time of the transition narration and the background color and even add effects.

To add a transition narration, simply click any video in the Library and click the *Title* button on the *Home* tab (just like adding an Opening Title) and a new five-second video will be added before the selected video. The default, once again, is white text on a black background.

Add as many transition narrations as you like; you can easily add them in front of every video in your Library if you wish to have a bit of text explaining the upcoming scene.

Benefits of Text in Your Movies

Your movies likely have sound, imagery, and action, and often that's all you need for a great movie. But text allows you to help your viewers in many ways:

- Dates and times: Text is useful for providing your viewer with a timeframe for what they are viewing. Is this last year's vacation, or five years ago? Is that a sunrise or sunset we're watching?

- List of items: For my worktable movie, I'll be providing a short video that lists the individual parts (and dimensions) used in its assembly.

- Points of interest: Small bits of text can be used to direct your viewer's attention to certain spots in a scene ("Watch the man's ice cream," "Here it comes, ..." "Splat!")

- Acknowledgments: In addition to the closing credits, text can be used to thank individuals and organizations for their support.

- Change of scenery: When your movie jumps from one place to another, text can be a big help to your viewers by telling them where the next scene takes place ("The Louvre, 2009" or "Space Mountain, Disney World").

By combining text with all the other elements you've learned so far (animation, visual effects, background music, voice-overs, and trimming), you can take your movies from homemade and amateur looking to polished and professional.

What's Next?

Now that you've got your movie edited, it's time to save your work and find a format that can be viewed by others. Fortunately, Movie Maker offers a variety of methods for making your hard work available to the world. Chapter 8 is going to show you how easy it is to immediately share your new movie with anyone or everyone.

Chapter 8

Saving a Movie

After all your hard work — cropping videos, adding background music and voice-overs, throwing in some animations and visual effects, and then adding some opening and closing credits — it'd be a shame to lose it all to a power outage, dead hard drive, or the fast fingers of a two and a half year old who really likes your shiny laptop (my son loves the clickety-clack of the buttons).

Fortunately, saving your work in Movie Maker is extremely simple and fast. If you've ever tried to close down Movie Maker, you've most likely received the alert window reminding you to save your project. But there's a difference between your movie project and the actual movie that viewers will watch. I'll explain those differences shortly.

In addition to saving your work as you continue to refine the final movie, you'll also eventually need to save the project files in a format that is playable on other devices, such as computers, laptops, phones, and other handheld devices. But again, this is all extremely easy to do if you understand the options available to you.

So, let's take this opportunity to go over the basics of saving your work. I'm going to show you how to save your work in-progress and then show you how to save your final masterpiece, or at least something that others can watch.

Saving a Movie Project

As you import videos into the Library and begin your work — editing, adding animations, and the like — you're going to want to save your project frequently. This is just standard computer practice, so you don't lose any of the work you've performed on your movie project.

There are two best practices here for saving. One is to save after small (or large) bits of work that you've performed, even if you are not finished with Movie Maker for the moment. For example, if you've just done a good bit of cropping on two videos in your Library, go ahead and save the work before beginning the editing work on the next video. Another good time to save is after applying some text to a scene and adding an animation or visual effect. As you'll see shortly, it only takes about two seconds to save your work to that point, and then you can get back to the next scene.

The second time to save is when you're done using Movie Maker. If you've finished your movie and are ready to share it with others, you still need to save the project before moving on to the steps to save the actual movie in a presentable format. If you find yourself needing to tackle other things (laundry, a television show, or maybe your real job), you'll need to save your project so you can return to it at a later time and pick up where you left off. Once again, you'll find that it takes only a few seconds to save your project until next time.

So, how exactly do you save your movie project? Simple. Figure 8-1 shows the File menu drop-down and the options that we need to use.

Figure 8-1. The File menu contains the Save Project and Save Project As options.

If you've not yet saved a project, select *Save Project* from the *File* menu. Figure 8-2 shows the screen that appears.

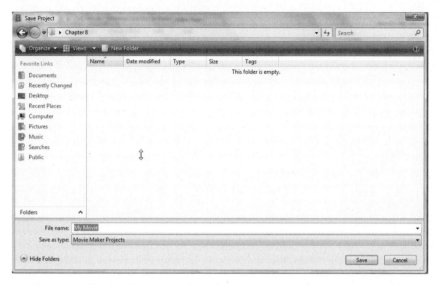

Figure 8-2. The Save Project window allows you to name your movie project file.

The *Save Project* window opens; you'll use this window to type in a name for your movie project (short but descriptive is always good) and browse to a location on your hard drive where you'll store the files. Click the *Save* button when you're done.

Easy, wasn't it? Now, let's suppose I go and add some text to the movie and a few animations. I'd like to save my progress, and Movie Maker offers me two options for doing so. The first is selecting *Save Project* again from the *File* menu. This time, however, I won't get the *Save Project* window seen in Figure 8-2. Instead, Movie Maker will simply save my changes to the project file I created in Figure 8-2. This method takes two clicks: click the *File* menu, and then click the *Save Project* option. But there's an even faster way.

If you're in a hurry to get back to your movie project, you can save yourself a click and simply use the *Save* button on the Movie Maker toolbar along the very top of the screen, just above the *Home* tab. Click the *Save* button as indicated in Figure 8-3 and get back to work.

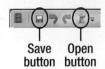

Save   Open
button button

Figure 8-3. The Save and Open buttons on the toolbar.

That's it! That's how easy and fast it is to save your work and prevent any loss of editing. You can use the *Save* button as often as you like (or the *Save Project* option from the *File* menu).

But what about that *Save Project As* option back in Figure 8-2? Well, there are two instances when that option will be useful to you.

Let's say that you've cropped all but one long video in the Library. You're just not sure about the right amount of editing you wish to apply to this video. You'd like to have a longer and shorter version of the video in your final movie, but you'd like some friends and family to watch both versions and help you decide. Well, the function of the *Save Project As* option is to allow you to save your current movie project under a different name. So, if your current movie project is titled "Summer in Madrid," you could select the *Save Project As* option, rename the project "Summer In Madrid (Long)," and finish up the movie with a longer version of that video.

But before you do any work on the long version, select *Save Project As* again and rename "Summer in Madrid (Long)" as "Summer in Madrid (Short)" and click Save. Now you have three movie projects on your hard drive:

1. Summer in Madrid

2. Summer in Madrid (Long)

3. Summer in Madrid (Short)

You can open the Short project and edit that last video down as much as you like without worrying that you've cut away too much. Use the *Save* button to save your work (obviously) and when you're done, close the project down. Next, click the *Open* button shown in Figure 8-3, open the long version, and perform your edits.

ExplainED

You can also add version numbers to your videos; project files with names of "Madrid version 1," "Madrid version 2," and Madrid version 3" all will work fine, but it may not be easy to remember what changes there are from one version to the next. While version numbers are more helpful when making small, subtle changes between projects, descriptive project names will ultimately be more useful to you.

Why do I have three versions of the project instead of just two? What happens if I show both the long and short versions to my friends, and they don't like either? What if the short version is too short, and the long is too long? Well, having the original "Summer in Madrid" project means I can start over with my editing with that full-length video ready for some new cropping.

ExplainED

To open a video project, click the Open button that looks like a small folder to the right of the Save button. If you don't see the Open button, click the down-pointing chevron and select "Open" to have a check placed beside it; the Open button will now appear on the small toolbar above the Home tab.

The *Save Project As* option is very useful, and you should take advantage of it as often as possible. Having the ability to return to a previous version of a project can save you tons of time that might otherwise be taken up with removing animations, text, and music.

Get in the habit of saving your projects often. Use a combination of *Save Project* and *Save Project As* to help you build your final movie and save time when reverting to a previous version.

NotED

Use the Save Project As option to divide your movie project into different editing versions. For example, save one (or more) projects that contains all the videos after they've been cropped. Save another project after you've added in background music. Save yet another project after you've added in text (or animations). If you decide at a later time that you don't like some part of your final movie (say you like the text, for example, but you like the music), then all you've got to do is open the project that has the cropping and music already saved and redo your text.

Final Movie Formats

Before you share or publish your movies with others, there are a few more decisions that have to be made. When it comes to displaying your final movie, you're going to need to know a little bit more about how it will be viewed by your audience.

NotED

Sharing and Publishing are two different things in Movie Maker. Sharing your movies refers to how you will provide them to viewers. Will it be email? Internet? CD or DVDs? Publishing refers to uploading your movies to Internet sites that host movies such as YouTube. I'll cover Publishing options in Chapter 9. Sharing options are covered later in this chapter.

Will your movie be played on a television or computer screen? Will it be played in high-definition format (16:9) or Standard (4:3)? Will it be sent via email as an attachment?

These are just a few of the decisions you'll need to make in order to properly save your movie in a format that is useful to a viewer. Fortunately, Movie Maker has made it very simple to save your final movie in various formats by placing all the possible decisions in a single location.

Click the *File* menu again and hover your mouse pointer over the *Save Movie* option, as shown in Figure 8-4.

Figure 8-4. Final movie formatting options in the Save Movie sub-menu .

The list of options available to you includes:

- High-definition (1080p)
- Burn a DVD
- High-definition (720p)
- Widescreen (480p)
- Standard-definition
- For portable device or mobile phone
- For email or instant messaging

I'm going to cover all of these options in the following sections (with the exception of "Burn a DVD," which I'll cover in Chapter 10). Read over them so you understand when to use one over another. And it's very possible you may choose to save your final movie in multiple formats (email and high-definition, for example) to offer your viewers different ways to watch your movie; this is a great way to make sure that no one misses out on your movie because they lack a particular method for viewing. (Not everyone has a high-definition television, but most have an email address, right?)

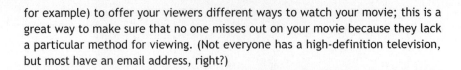

NotED

Some format options may appear to be available to you, but may not actually work depending on the format of the original video taken with a video recorder. If you are not using a high-definition video recorder, you can choose the high-definition option, but the quality of the final movie will not be displayed in actual high-definition.

High-definition (1080p)

The high-definition (1080p) option offers the best viewing quality, but it comes with a price. Actually, it comes with a few prices.

First, the final movie file will be very large in file size. HD1080p movies are not something you'll be able to email a friend as an attachment. And it's likely not going to be quick (or easy) to transfer them to a friend's computer using a pen drive.

Second, high-definition movies are best displayed on computer screens that support 1080p. This is an industry standard (right now) for high-definition televisions, but not all computer screens (LCDs) can handle the high-quality images. If you're going to be displaying this movie on your high-definition computer screen, then by all means, choose this option. But if you wish to share your movie with others, you need to make certain that viewers have access to a high-definition screen that supports a 1920 × 1080 pixel display.

The high-definition (1080p) option, when selected, will allow you to name your movie file and choose a location to store it.

LinkED

The technical explanations of high-definition and terms such as 1080p and 720p could fill books in themselves. If you wish to know more about high-definition standards, please visit http://en.wikipedia.org/wiki/720p and http://en.wikipedia.org/wiki/1080p for more detailed discussions.

A five-minute video saved in high-definition (1080p) would be approximately 285MB in size.

High-definition (720p)

As with the high-definition (1080p) option, the 720p option should only be selected when you know your viewers will be able to view the final movie on a screen that supports the 720p standard. The final resolution of the displayed movie will be 1280 × 720 pixels.

This option also saves your movie file to your hard drive using the WMV format, but the image quality will be lower when compared to 1080p. The file size will be lower, obviously, but HD720p files are still not capable of being sent via email as an attachment.

The 720p option is a fairly safe one to select, however, if you know your viewer will be watching it on a computer LCD screen (also known as a flat screen).

A five-minute video saved in high-definition (720p) would be approximately 215MB in size.

Widescreen (480p)

The widescreen (480p) format is best known as the format for early plasma television screens. While new plasma screens support the latest 1080p format, if you or your viewers have an older plasma screen, this is one format option that is available that still provides a nice image. The final resolution of the displayed movie will be 720 × 480 pixels.

When saving a final movie in the 480p format, it will be displayed in widescreen (16:9) format. This means that if you shot the video using a video recorder that records in 4:3 format, the movie will be displayed with black bars to the right and left of the screen to compensate for the widescreen display.

A five-minute video saved in Widescreen (480p) would be approximately 105MB in size.

Standard-definition

The standard-definition format will display your movie using the 4:3 display ratio found on standard non-widescreen televisions. The final resolution of the displayed movie will also be 640 × 480 pixels.

This is one of the safest formats to select when you know your viewers will be watching your movie on a computer screen but are unsure about the type/resolution of display they are using.

The file size is substantially lower based on movies of similar length saved in any of the high-definition formats. Still, the standard-definition format is not recommended for use when sending the movie via email.

ExplainED

Even though there is an option for portable devices (see the next section), the standard-definition format will work with many of the newer portable devices. These devices are coming standard with tons of hard drive space or static memory (as well as the ability to add more memory using a memory card).

A five-minute video saved in standard-definition would be approximately 105MB in size. (Standard-definition movies are approximately the same size as widescreen movies.)

For Portable Device or Mobile Phone

Portable devices, such as the iPhone or the iPods, that support video are everywhere. But it's not just Apple devices; there are thousands of handheld phones and other electronic devices that are capable of playing video.

For these devices, the movie being displayed isn't going to have the highest resolution, and often the images will appear slightly grainy and choppy. Until portable devices improve, however, you'll likely want to use this option for saving your final movie if you intend to provide it to viewers who are using portable devices.

The file sizes are relatively small compared to the high-definition and standard formats, and these files are easy to move around using a simple USB flash drive. For shorter videos, you may even be able to email movies using this format. The resolution of movies saved in this format is 320×240 pixels.

A five-minute video saved using the Portable devices option would be approximately 60MB in size.

For Email or Instant Messaging

For the ultimate in compact movie size, Movie Maker offers you the option to save your movie in 320 × 240 resolution; the same resolution found for the portable device format, but with a much lower quality when it comes to color and sound.

Still, if you've got a small movie that you need to share with others via email, this is the best option available. You can easily save the movie in better formats for anyone wanting a more detailed version, but the email/instant messaging format is great for sharing a video quickly with friends and family.

A five-minute video saved using the email/instant messaging option would be approximately 10MB in size.

Saving the Final Movie

Now it's time to save your movie. As I wrote earlier, Movie Maker makes this extremely simple. Just click the *File* menu, select the *Save Movie* option, and choose one of the format options discussed in the previous section.

As you hover your mouse pointer over a format option, you'll notice a small grey box appear. This box contains some useful information for you, including the resolution of the final video as well as an estimate of the file size (based on the length of your movie).

NotED

You may see something called bit rate (in addition to the estimated file size) when choosing a format option (see Figure 8-5). This is simply a rate, given in megabits per second, which can be used to calculate a more accurate file size for your movies. If your movie is 26 seconds in length, you can multiply that value by the bit rate to get a final file size. The estimated file size (see Figure 8-5) can also be used to calculate file size based on the per-minute length of your videos, but bit rate will be more accurate.

For example, in Figure 8-5, I want to use the portable device option, so I'm hovering my mouse pointer over it.

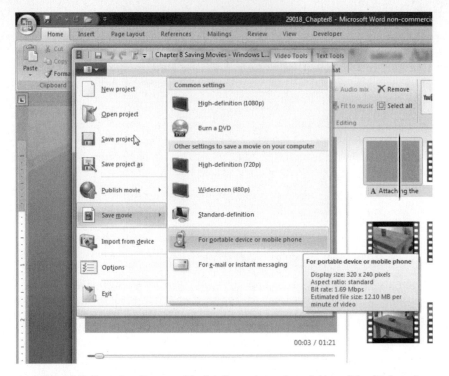

Figure 8-5. Format options provide details on size and resolution of the final movie.

Notice that the screen shown in Figure 8-5 tells me that my final movie will be displayed with a resolution of 320 × 240 pixels. It's also going to be displayed using the standard aspect ratio (4:3) and the file size will be approximately 12MB per minute. My video is almost a minute and a half, so the file size should be no larger than 18MB.

ExplainED

The file size is just an estimate. You won't know the exact file size until after you save your movie. If the file size is larger than you desire (or can use), you'll need to either crop your movie some more or save it in a smaller file size format (such as the email format).

After selecting the portable device option, I see a window like the one in Figure 8-6.

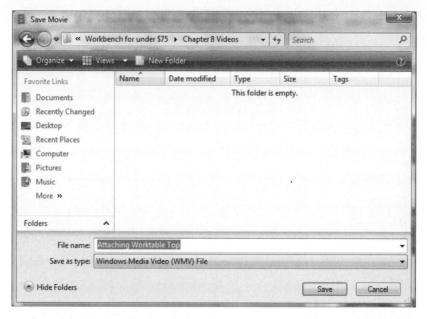

Figure 8-6. Provide a filename and location for saving your newly formatted movie.

Notice that the title of this window is *Save Movie*, not *Save Project*. After I click the *Save* button, all the editing, music, text, and special effects that I've worked with in the movie project will be combined into a single video (versus the multiple videos I imported into the Library) that I've titled "Attaching Worktable Top."

ExplainED

If you're wondering why this movie focuses on just attaching the worktable top and not building the entire worktable, it's because I'm creating multiple movies, each covering a different aspect of the worktable construction. I'll be taking all these individual movies (from different movie projects that I've saved) and putting them on a DVD in Chapter 10. Movie Maker allows you to make a DVD, complete with a menu system that allows the viewer to select from multiple movies and watch only what they wish to watch. Instead of forcing my viewers to watch a single, 30-minute movie, I can offer them four or five smaller movies using a menu system, and let them watch one or all of them at their leisure and in any order they wish.

You'll see a window appear like the one in Figure 8-7; it's a simple percentage bar that tells you how far along the saving process has progressed.

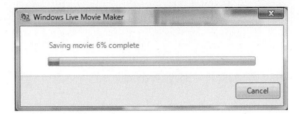

Figure 8-7. The bar tells you how much of the movie has been created.

NotED

For large movies, the saving process could take a while. This is especially true if you are saving your movie in one of the high-definition formats. The saving process can put a large demand on your hard drive and processor, so I recommend that you not try and do any other work on your computer while the progress bar is displayed. Take a break and come back to check on the progress; I've had movies take up to 30 minutes or longer to save, so don't be surprised if it takes a long time. It's normal.

When the saving process is complete, you'll see a new window appear, like the one shown in Figure 8-8, that offers you the ability to play the movie or open the folder where the movie is stored.

Figure 8-8. You'll be alerted when your saved movie is ready for viewing.

Clicking the *Open folder* button opens up the folder where the movie is stored, as seen in Figure 8-9.

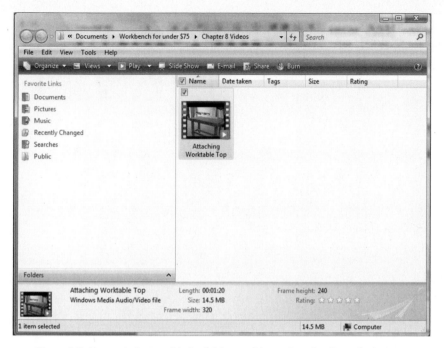

Figure 8-9. My movie is stored in its folder, and I can view details at the bottom.

Select your movie by clicking once on it, and you'll be able to view details along the bottom of the window. Here I can see that my movie is 80 seconds long and is 14.5MB in size.

To watch it, I simply double-click the video. Figure 8-10 shows my movie playing.

I'd like to save another version of this movie for emailing to my friends, so I select the *File* menu, click *Save Movie,* and then choose the email format option. Figure 8-11 shows how I've added "email" to the end of the filename to indicate this video is suitable as an attachment. (You can also see the original movie file sitting in the folder in Figure 8-11).

Figure 8-10. Watch your movies by launching them directly from your computer.

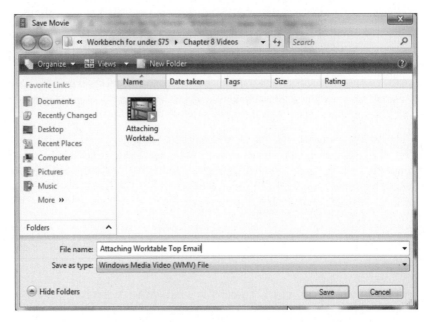

Figure 8-11. Save as many different versions of the movie as you like.

After the movie has been saved, I click it once to view the file information as seen in Figure 8-12.

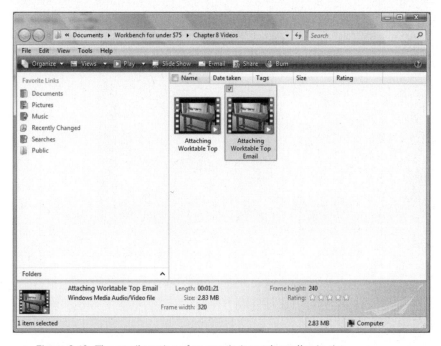

Figure 8-12. The email version of my movie is much smaller in size.

As you can see, the movie is still 80 seconds in length, but the file size is now only 2.83MB in size. That's a perfect size for emailing as an attachment. But what does it look like?

After double-clicking the file, Figure 8-13 shows what is displayed.

Well, the display screen is the same size, but there are some slight differences. It's difficult to tell from Figure 8-13, but the email version of my movie has a grainy image quality that isn't as detailed as the portable device version. The sound is also slightly more "tinny;" it sounds like I'm speaking through a tube and there's a hollow, echo-y sound. Again, it's hard to describe, so my best suggestion is to just try it with your own movie and see if you can live with the results.

Figure 8-13. The email version of my movie plays.

NotED

When you choose the email format, you're sacrificing sound and visual quality for reduced file size. There's always going to be give and take when it comes to saving your movies. The higher the video and sound quality, the larger the file size. But because most email hosting services put a limit on attachments of between 5MB and 10MB these days, you're typically going to be limited to the email format if you wish to send out your movie via email.

Sharing Digital Movies

I'll be talking about making your movies available to others over the Internet and via a DVD in Chapters 9 and 10 respectively. It's obviously much easier to share your movies with others (especially large and/or high-definition files) if you upload them to a video hosting service (such as YouTube, covered in Chapter 9) or hand someone a DVD disc to play on their computer or DVD player.

But what if you lack the capability to burn a DVD? What if you use dial-up Internet service instead of broadband (hi-speed) Internet? How can you share your movies with others?

Well, there are the following three methods that I can think of:

1. Email (which was discussed in the previous section)

2. Burning your movies to CD (if you have a CD burner)

3. Copying your movies to a USB flash drive

All three options, however, are dependent on the size of your final movie's file. Sending a movie by email has two limitations: your email host provider will likely limit you to 5MB or maybe 10MB attachments, but keep in mind that your recipient(s) may be limited to 2MB by a different email host provider.

If you have a 1GB USB flash drive and your movie is 2GB in size, you're not going to be able to transfer it from computer to computer using that particular method.

LinkED

are applications you can download and install that will split large files into smaller "chunks." These smaller files can then be reassembled on the destination hard drive; this may require that the same application be installed on the destination computer. Some file splitting applications add the ability to reassemble automatically on the destination computer without installing the file splitting application. Visit http://www.snapfiles.com/Freeware/downloader/fwfilesplit.html and you'll find a nice selection of freeware file splitting applications to test.

Burning your movie to a CD is another option, but a CD will hold a maximum of 700MB (650MB is typical). But again, if your movie is larger in size than 700MB, you'll either need to buy and use a DVD burner (which can hold a maximum of 4GB on a single-sided DVD disc; 8GB on a dual-side) or reduce the size of your movie by selecting a format with lower quality and file size characteristics.

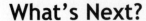
What's Next?

So your movie is saved and you're ready to share it with the world. Well, you have options. Two of the more popular methods are burning your movies to a DVD (covered in Chapter 10) or uploading your movie to various movie sites on the Internet. In Chapter 9, I'm going to show you how easy it is to upload your final movie to YouTube, the most popular movie-hosting site in the world. It's not the only movie-hosting site, however, so I'll also show you how to configure Movie Maker for a few other popular sites.

Chapter 9

Publishing a Movie

Congratulations! You've completed your movie, and now you want to share it with the world. Who wouldn't? All that hard work — editing, cropping, voice-overs, animations, and text narration — should be on display.

Fortunately, Movie Maker has made sharing your movie a very simple task. I'm not kidding: with just a few clicks and a sign-in, your movie will be available for viewing to anyone with an Internet connection.

Publishing your movie is just as important as all the previous work you've done — choosing the proper method for sharing your movie is an important decision, so I'm also going to provide you with some things to think over before you actually put your movie out there for the world to watch, review, and tell their friends about.

So, let's get started. I'm going to walk you through the process of uploading your movie with one of the biggest names in video sharing: YouTube. When we're done, you'll have the know-how to share your future movies with anyone and everyone.

YouTube.com

If you've never heard of YouTube.com, I'm very surprised. It's the single largest provider of both amateur and professional videos and movies on the Internet. You can find home movies, how-to videos, television shows (not all, but many), commentaries, documentaries, and stuff that's just too strange to classify.

Fortunately, YouTube.com has some heavy-duty search and filtering tools available that help visitors to the Web site find exactly what they're looking for, whatever that may be. That said, the search and filtering tools are useless if users (like you) upload movies without any information about your movie. I'll get into that a bit later when I show you how to upload a movie, but for now I need you to understand that the key to getting your movie viewed is to give YouTube visitors a way to actually find your movie among the estimated millions of movies in its database.

ExplainED

There doesn't seem to be an official response to the question of how many movies/videos that YouTube hosts. In 2009, YouTube did announce that 20 hours of video is uploaded every single minute (yes, every 60 seconds), so that should give you some idea of how much video content is being added to its database.

YouTube will allow you to watch videos for free: no subscription fees or costs incurred. You can also upload videos for free, but you do have to create a YouTube user account (more on that shortly). After creating an account, you can upload videos to your heart's content.

LinkED

YouTube does have quite a few restrictions — you cannot upload copyrighted material, such as a digital recording of your favorite television show, for example. For a complete list of its standards, visit www.youtube.com/t/community_guidelines and read carefully. YouTube can remove movies at any time, without any explanation. Some violations will even be reported to the authorities, so please be careful what you choose to upload.

YouTube does have competitors (Google Videos is a big one — even though Google owns YouTube, it still has Google Videos to offer search capabilities that aren't available with YouTube), so don't think you're limited to just YouTube for sharing your movies. But there is a benefit to using Movie Maker and having a YouTube user account — Movie Maker allows you to seamlessly upload your finished movies from within Movie Maker with a few clicks of your mouse. That simplicity is a strong argument for considering sharing your movies via YouTube.

And that's exactly what I'm going to show you. First, I'm going to walk you through creating a YouTube user account, and then I'm going to show you how easy it is to share a movie using Movie Maker's built-in YouTube Upload feature.

Creating a YouTube User Account

If you already have a YouTube user account, feel free to skip to the next section, "Uploading Movies to YouTube via Movie Maker." But if not, take a few minutes to read over the following, and then set up your YouTube user account.

First, open Movie Maker and the movie project you wish to upload. Figure 9-1 shows my movie project, complete with animations, text, and editing.

Figure 9-1. Publishing a movie to YouTube can be done from within Movie Maker.

ExplainED

Uploading a movie to YouTube via Movie Maker is done using a movie project, not a final movie file that you saved (see Chapter 8). You can upload a final movie that you've saved to YouTube, but you do that by visiting YouTube.com and logging in to upload a finished movie.

Next, click *File* and select "*Publish movie.*" A fly-out menu will appear, like the one seen in Figure 9-2. Click "*Publish on YouTube*" to continue. (You can also click the YouTube icon on the Home tab.)

Figure 9-2. Use the File menu to publish a movie on YouTube.

A YouTube login window will appear, like the one shown in Figure 9-3. Enter your YouTube username and password, click *Sign In*, and then skip ahead to the next section, "Uploading a Movie to YouTube via Movie Maker."

Figure 9-3. Sign in to YouTube with your username and password.

If you don't yet have a YouTube user account, click the link labeled "*Don't have an account? Create one.*"

A new web browser window will open with instructions for creating a user account, as shown in Figure 9-4.

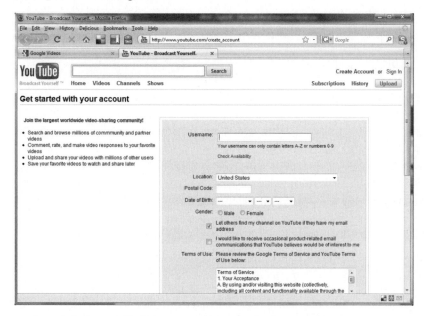

Figure 9-4. Create a YouTube user account to upload your movies.

Follow the instructions carefully. When you are done, you'll need to check your e-mail for a message from YouTube. Follow the instructions in the e-mail to verify your new account.

When done, close the browser window and return to the YouTube login screen in Movie Maker. Enter your username and password and click the *Sign In* button. After signing in, you'll see a screen like the one shown in Figure 9-5.

Figure 9-5. Provide some information on your movie before publishing.

The *Title* field is already filled in with the name of the movie project, but you can change this easily enough. I'll replace "Chapter 9 Publishing Movies" with "Worktable Part 4" to indicate this is part of a video series.

For the *Description* field, feel free to write a few sentences about the video. This is text that the viewer can read to learn more about your movie. Feel free to include information such as the date or location of a movie. But don't include personal information such as e-mail addresses or full names.

The *Tags* field is another useful and important section of the "*Publish on YouTube*" window. Visitors to YouTube can use keywords (such as "worktable") to search for videos of interest. Later I'll show you how to add more words to help viewers find your movies, but for now a few words that relate to your movie should be sufficient.

Be sure to click the *Category* drop-down menu and select a suitable category that describes your movie. I'll select "How-to & Style," but "Education" could also be used.

Under the *Permission* drop-down menu, select Public or Private. For now, select Public, and I'll show you later how to change this back to Private if you don't want everyone to have access to it.

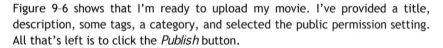

The Private setting is useful for sharing videos only with friends and family. The Public setting makes your video available to anyone with Internet and YouTube access.

Figure 9-6 shows that I'm ready to upload my movie. I've provided a title, description, some tags, a category, and selected the public permission setting. All that's left is to click the *Publish* button.

Figure 9-6. Provide details about your movie and click the Publish button.

After clicking the *Publish* button, you'll see a progress bar like the one in Figure 9-7. Before your video is published, it is saved in a format that YouTube allows. Don't worry if you haven't selected a format (see Chapter 8); YouTube will select the best fit.

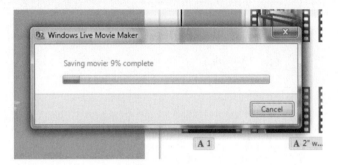

Figure 9-7. The bar tells you how much of the movie has been saved.

After the video is saved, you'll see another bar that tells you how far along the publishing process has moved. This is shown in Figure 9-8.

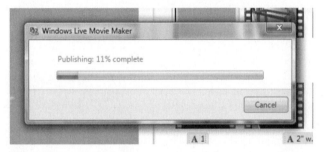

Figure 9-8. The bar tells you how much of the movie has been published.

ExplainED

Depending on your Internet connection speed, this could take a while. For short movies, it might only take a minute or longer. For my two-minute movie, however, it took about seven minutes on a wireless Internet connection. Just be aware that the publishing process could take a while for long movies.

When your movie has completed the publishing process, you will see a window appear, telling you your video has been successfully uploaded. Figure 9-9 shows that screen.

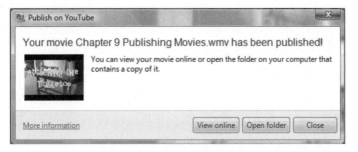

Figure 9-9. Congratulations on publishing your movie!

Go ahead and click the "*View online*" button, and a new browser window will open. Your movie will be played, as shown in Figure 9-10.

ExplainED

You may have noticed that the screen in Figure 9-9 tells me that "Chapter 9 Publishing Movies.wmv" has been published. That's the name of the file of my movie project. Figure 9-10 shows the title of the movie that matches the one I entered in Figure 9-6.

Notice in Figure 9-10 that your username is displayed in the right column, with the description of the movie below it. Right below the description, you'll see a text box labeled URL; copy and paste that text into an e-mail, for example, and the recipient of that e-mail can click the link and be taken immediately to your newly uploaded movie.

Figure 9-10. Your movie begins to play on YouTube.com.

NotED

The Embed option is HTML text that can be pasted into Web sites. This puts a YouTube video player on the screen, allowing visitors to other Web sites to watch a video without having to leave the current site for YouTube.com.

And that's how you publish a movie. But I'm not done yet. There's a bit more to show you, so keep the browser window open that is displaying your movie. In the next section, I'm going to show you a few additional settings you may want to configure for your videos.

LinkED

You can watch the movie I've uploaded by visiting www.youtube.com/watch?v=n76XEHw8lD0&feature=youtube_gdata.

YouTube Movie Settings

Once you've uploaded your movie, you could easily move on to your next project. But YouTube offers some additional options and features to a video owner that I think are worth a brief mention.

If you're not still viewing your uploaded movie's page (see Figure 9-10), go ahead and log back in to YouTube.

Along the top of the screen, you'll see your login name with a small downward pointing arrow next to it. Move your mouse pointer over your name or the triangle and select *My Videos,* as shown in Figure 9-11.

Figure 9-11. A shortcut to viewing all the movies you've uploaded to YouTube.

You'll be taken to a screen like the one seen in Figure 9-12. This is a collection of all the movies you've uploaded to YouTube.

For all of your movies, you have many options available from this screen. For example, you can play your movie (click the Play button) and edit tags and the description (and more) by clicking the Edit button.

Figure 9-12. Your movies are listed, along with many control buttons.

NotED

I encourage you to check out all the other buttons available to you; the Captions button, for example, will allow you to add blocks of text anywhere in your movies to provide additional information for your viewers. To learn about all the options, simply click a button and you'll be taken to a new screen where the feature is described. You'll always have the ability to cancel or return to the previous screen.

There are a couple of options on the Edit screen that I want to bring to your attention, so go ahead and click the *Edit* button, and you'll see a screen like the one in Figure 9-13.

The *Edit* button brings you to a screen with four tabs along the top edge: *Info & Settings*, *AudioSwap*, *Annotations*, and *Captions & Subtitles*. Feel free to click the other tabs to see what features they offer, but I'd like to bring your attention back to the *Info & Settings* screen, and point out that this is where you can edit the Title, Description, Tags, and Category for your video. Make any changes that you need, but don't close down this screen yet.

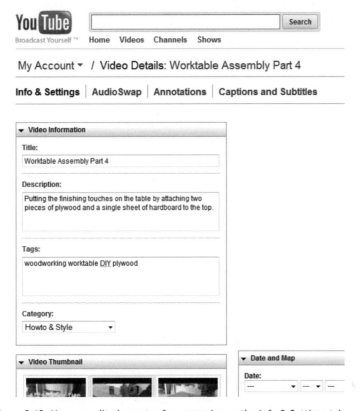

Figure 9-13. You can edit elements of your movies on the Info & Settings tab.

Scroll down the page and you'll see some additional options, as shown in Figure 9-14.

Take a look at the *Privacy* option. You have two choices here: Share or Private. Share is the default setting, and will allow anyone to view your movie. If you select the Private option, you can share your movie with no more than 25 people.

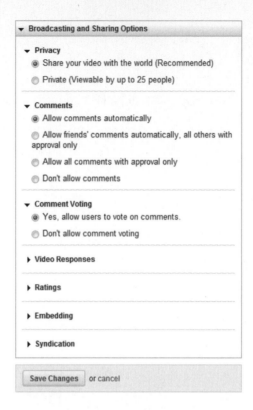

Figure 9-14. Additional options you can configure for your movies.

NotED

If you select the Private option, then put a check in the Limited Access URL box. You'll be given a URL/link that you can e-mail to your friends and family. YouTube doesn't care who clicks the link and watches the movie, so be careful about who receives the link. You might even include a request in your e-mail to not share the link with anyone.

The *Comments* option is another important one. If your movie is available for everyone to view and you allow comments (the default selection), you're likely to find over time that some unsavory and not-so-friendly comments will be posted in response to your movie. This is one of the drawbacks to sharing your movie with the world. If this bothers you, do what I do: select "Don't allow comments" and move on. I'm not concerned about comments on my uploaded videos. I send my family links to my videos, and I'd rather them not have to deal with bad language and insults in the comment section. Ultimately, it's your call.

Other options allow you to enable or disable many things — the rating system, the ability to embed your video into other Web sites, and even the ability to view your movies on mobile phones.

To the right of the screen, you can add information about the location of your movie, as shown in Figure 9-15.

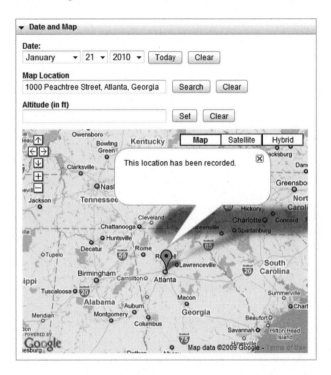

Figure 9-15. Information about the location of your movie can be helpful to viewers.

NotED

Many videos could benefit from location information. For example, suppose you've uploaded a video of a whitewater rafting trip you've just completed. It would be helpful to viewers to indicate on the map in Figure 9-15 where your adventure started (or ended). You can also mark locations of museums, vacation spots, and other special events where viewers might like to schedule their own visit.

When you're done with your edits, be sure to click the *Save Changes* button at the bottom of the screen.

The services that YouTube provides are too numerous to cover in a single chapter. I encourage you to spend some time looking around YouTube to see what other options are available.

LinkED

Be sure to check out the YouTube Handbook. It's got tips and tricks for making the most of the online video service. You can find it at www.youtube.com/t/yt_handbook_home.

More Video Hosting Sites

In addition to YouTube, Movie Maker supports a few other video hosting services. Click the File menu and select Publish movie. From the fly-out menu, click "Add a plug-in," as shown in Figure 9-16.

Figure 9-16. Additional video hosting services are available in Movie Maker.

A new browser window will open, like the one seen in Figure 9-17.

It's a short list, but it does appear to be growing. Video hosting services can create plug-ins that allow Movie Maker to easily upload videos without having to exit the Movie Maker application.

For example, if you have a Facebook account, click the "LiveUpload to Facebook" to add this plug-in. Once the plug-in is installed, you'll be able to upload videos directly to your Facebook account from within Movie Maker, instead of having to log in to Facebook and use its tools to upload movies.

If you've got a Picasa account (for uploading photos and videos), you can likewise click the Picasa Web Publisher plug-in to give Movie Maker the ability to upload your movies directly to the Picasa service.

Figure 9-17. Click a video hosting service to download and install it.

LinkED

If you're not familiar with Facebook, visit www.facebook.com to learn more. It's a hugely popular (and free) service that makes keeping in touch with friends, family members, and co-workers extremely simple and fun.

The Picasa Web Service is another popular hosting site for videos and photos — you can find more information by visiting http://picasa.google.com/intl/en/features.html.

If you have a video hosting service that you use and it's not listed on this page, e-mail this link (http://blogs.msdn.com/pix/pages/Plug_2D00_ins.aspx) to your hosting service and ask them to consider having a plug-in created. If they are willing to do so, you'll have a fast and reliable method for uploading your movies directly to your hosting site using Movie Maker.

What's Next?

YouTube is great for hosting single videos, but it does require a connection to the Internet. But what if you want to offer your viewers multiple videos? Or what if they don't have an Internet connection? Fortunately, Movie Maker also offers you the ability to add your videos to a DVD (it's called burning a DVD). And if you've got multiple videos you want to put on the DVD, Movie Maker even offers you the ability to create an eye-catching menu system, just like real DVD movies offer. Keep reading, because Chapter 10 is all about DVD authoring, and viewers of your videos are sure to be impressed.

Chapter 10

Creating a DVD

In Chapter 9, I showed you how to publish your movies with YouTube. It's a great way to enable others to see your movies. And in Chapter 8, I showed you how to save your movies in various formats, depending on how you were going to share them: e-mail or a portable device (such as a flash drive) were a few of the options available to you.

But there are drawbacks to these methods. With e-mail, for example, you can't send very large videos. Movies of 5MB or 10MB are typically no longer than a minute or two, and the resolution is very grainy. A flash drive requires a computer with a USB port to view or save the movies to a hard drive. And while YouTube doesn't limit you on video size or resolution, it does require a high-speed Internet connection. What happened to sharing your movies the old-fashioned way, on DVD?

Well, it's alive and kicking (but does require that your computer have a DVD burner). Movie Maker offers you the ability to take your movies and create a DVD that you can deliver to friends, family, business contacts ... anyone who has a DVD player or a DVD drive in their computer. And best of all, Movie Maker offers you the ability to create a cool menu system, so your viewers can see what's on the DVD and select only what they wish to view.

Now you no longer have to force your viewers to watch your 85-minute long vacation video of scene change after scene change after scene change. Instead, they can select from your 15 smaller movies with titles such as, "Day at the Beach," "The Trip Home," and "Our Day Hike."

Best of all, this isn't difficult to do. Movie Maker handles all the complicated tasks for you, requiring you to simply know the location of your individual movie files that you saved (see Chapter 8).

Throughout this book, I've been creating small videos that show various parts of my worktable assembly. I've collected all those individual movie files, and I'm ready to create a DVD to share with my friends. So, follow along in the next

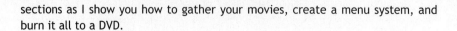

sections as I show you how to gather your movies, create a menu system, and burn it all to a DVD.

Gather Your Movies

Whether you have one movie or thirty, before you burn a DVD you're going to need to locate all your movie files. In the case of more than three or four movies, it will save time if you create a single "Burn to DVD" folder and copy all your movies to it. Once the DVD is burned, you can delete the "Burn to DVD folder."

ExplainED

If you lack enough hard drive space to make copies of all your movie files, this isn't a problem. You'll simply have to browse to all the movie file locations during the DVD creation process covered later in the chapter.

Figure 10-1 shows my temporary "Burn to DVD" folder, where I've saved four different movie files. You can tell by the titles of each movie what the video is about. I've also selected all four movies (hold down the Ctrl key and click each video) so I can see that the total movie size is 400MB — plenty of room on a single DVD disc!

ExplainED

Keep in mind that a standard DVD-R or DVD+R disc will hold a maximum of 4GB (gigabytes). If you have a lot of high-definition movies, you can fill up a single DVD fairly quickly. If you want to fit more movies onto a single DVD, you'll likely need to save your movie project files using a format that has lower resolution (try 720p or Widescreen instead of 1080p). Refer to Chapter 8 for a discussion on formats and file sizes.

Figure 10-1. Start by pulling your movie files together into a single location.

If you aren't able to pull all your movies together into a single folder, don't worry. When selecting movies to add to your DVD, you'll just have to browse to the various locations rather than a single folder. This likely won't be a big deal for a small group of movies, but if you've got ten, twenty or maybe forty small videos to add to a DVD, it could become tedious — just a warning.

Create Your DVD

Now I'm ready to start selecting the movies that will be added to the DVD. The procedure for doing this is a little odd; to start your DVD, you must open a movie project file, and it must be the project file containing the first movie you wish to add to your DVD.

Figure 10-2 shows that I've opened my project titled "The Inventory." This is the title of the first video I wish to offer for viewing on my DVD (but it can be changed a little later in the process if you decide you'd rather have a different video start the DVD).

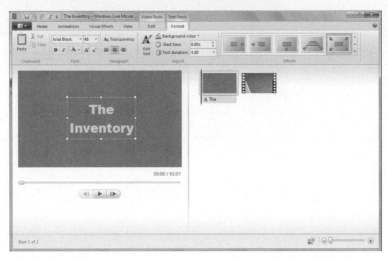

Figure 10-2. Open the first movie's project file to begin the DVD-creation process.

Next, click *File*, then select *"Save movie,"* and then click *"Burn a DVD"* from the fly-out menu, as shown in Figure 10-3.

Figure 10-3. Click "Burn a DVD" to begin creating your DVD.

A window will open that you can use to browse to the folder containing the first movie you wish to add to your DVD. In Figure 10-4, I've browsed to my "Burn to DVD" folder, which shows all four final movies ready to be added to the DVD.

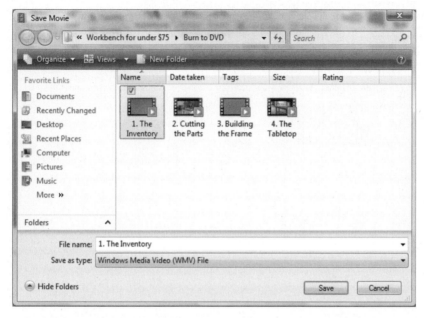

Figure 10-4. Save your final movie or select an existing one to be overwritten.

ExplainED

To get access to the "Burn a DVD" option, you must have a movie project loaded in Movie Maker. It really does matter which project you select, too, because you're going to end up saving it again (unless you've never saved it as a final movie, in which case here's your chance). After selecting the "Burn a DVD" option, you'll be able to provide a name for the final movie. If you've already saved the movie previously, just browse for it and select the original on your hard drive (as in Figure 10-4). You may be told that the movie already exists. That's okay, just click Yes when asked if you wish to replace it.

The movie project will be saved (see Chapter 8 for an explanation of the process: it may take a few minutes or more). After the final movie is saved, you'll see a new window open, like the one in figure 10-5.

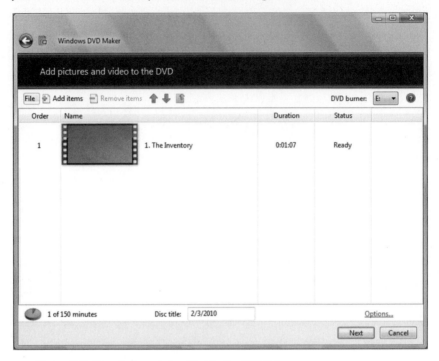

Figure 10-5. Your first movie is added to the DVD list.

Look carefully at Figure 10-5. Along the bottom of the window you'll see an estimate of how many minutes are left for adding movies (in this case, I've used just one of 150 minutes). I can also give the DVD a title by typing one in the "Disc title" box, or just leave it with the default date. There are a few other options, but I'll cover those later once we have a few more movies added.

ExplainED

The disc title is what will be displayed on the DVD menu's starting screen. I'll cover the menu system later in this chapter, but I do recommend changing the default date to something a bit more descriptive.

Now it's time to add some more movies. To do this, I simply click the *"Add items"* button, located near the top of Figure 10-5. This brings up a window like the one seen in Figure 10-4; I simply browse for and locate the next movie I wish to add. I'll do this for the remaining three movies. Figure 10-6 shows that I've now added all four movies for burning to a DVD.

ExplainED

You can hold down the Ctrl button and select multiple movies if they are located in the same folder. The movies are added in the order they are listed in the browse window, but you can easily shuffle them up or down using the "Move up" and "Move down" buttons, or dragging a video and dropping it in a new position. Movies stored in different folders will need to be added individually using the "Add items" button.

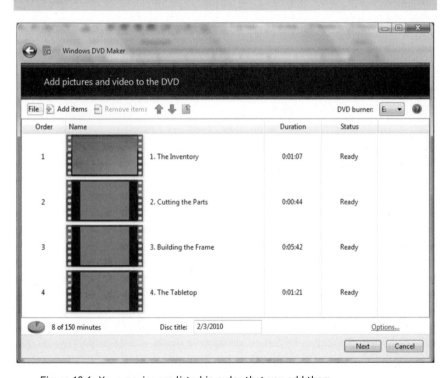

Figure 10-6. Your movies are listed in order that you add them.

You can easily rearrange the order of your movies by clicking a single movie and holding down the mouse button as you drag the movie up the list or down the list. Release the mouse button to move the movie. Repeat as often as necessary.

Before I click on the *Next* button in Figure 10-6 to continue to the DVD burning process, I'd like to explain the *Options* link also shown in that figure. Click the *Options* link and you'll see a window like the one in Figure 10-7.

Figure 10-7. DVD options are available by clicking the Options link.

Even if you've saved any or all of your movies in 16:9 format, you can override those default settings by selecting the 4:3 DVD aspect ratio on the DVD Options window. Likewise, if you want your Standard 4:3 aspect videos to be presented in 16:9 format, select that option here. (This will simply add black bars to the left and right of the videos, but it will prevent some televisions from distorting a video by stretching it to fit the widescreen format.)

You can also choose whether to have the DVD skip a menu system (see the next section) and start right into playing your video or videos. The option titled "Play video and end with DVD menu" will do just that. After your movies have played, the DVD menu will be displayed so your viewers can choose to go back and see a specific movie or watch them all again. The "Play video in a continuous loop" will just keep replaying your movies until the DVD is ejected.

Finally, you can control the DVD burning speed from this window. I recommend that you leave this option alone (as well as the Temporary File Location path) and allow Movie Maker to select the best option based on your computer's hardware.

NotED

The NTSC and PAL options are for saving a DVD for use in specific countries. For the United States, leave the setting as NTSC. If you'll be sending the DVD to a friend overseas (in Europe, for example), the PAL option is likely to be required. If you're unsure of which setting to choose, you'll need to do a little research (try Googling the country name along with they keywords PAL and NTSC) to determine the proper setting. You can also view the image located at http://en.wikipedia.org/ wiki/File:PAL-NTSC-SECAM.svg for a color-coded map showing each country and its default format.

Click the *OK* button to close the DVD Options window, and then click the *Next* button, as shown in Figure 10-6.

You'll now see the "*Ready to burn disc*" screen, shown in Figure 10-8. You can click the *Burn* button now to create the disc, but hold off on that for just a moment or you'll miss another nice feature of Movie Maker, the Menu creation system.

Figure 10-8. You can burn the disc now, or select and customize a DVD menu first.

Creating a DVD Menu

Creating a DVD menu is not only an eye-catching option for your DVD, but it also gives your viewers the ability to select from multiple movies on the disc and watch only what they wish to watch. If you have more than two or three movies burned to your DVD, this is a nice option to provide them. And Movie Maker, fortunately, provides a large selection of different menu looks and designs for you to choose from.

By default, the Full Screen menu is selected, as shown in Figure 10-8. Feel free to scroll up and down the list on the right side of the screen and click the menu options to see how they work. In Figure 10-9, I've selected the Reflections menu.

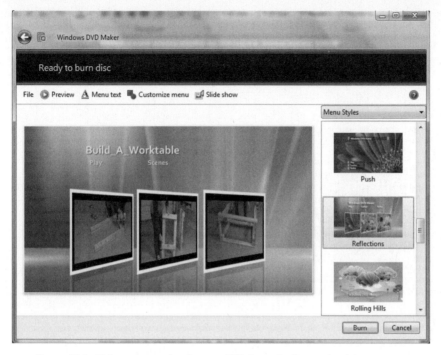

Figure 10-9. Pick a menu option for your DVD from the list on the right.

One really nice feature of Movie Maker is the ability to play around with the menu option you selected before burning the disc. Click the *Preview* button in the upper left-hand corner of the screen shown in Figure 10-9, and a virtual menu will be created, allowing you to play around with the controls: play, rewind, and so on. Figure 10-10 shows how my DVD menu will look if I choose the Reflections option.

Take note of the *Play* and *Scenes* options on the preview screen. These options are available on all the menu options you can select (see Figure 10-9). If you click the *Scenes* option with your mouse, you'll see a view that shows all the movies available on the disc. Figure 10-11 shows my four movies, including the opening title credits I created for each.

Figure 10-10. A preview of my DVD menu system.

NotED

This is an example of why it's good to add opening titles to your movies. Without them, the menu system only displays a small animation taken from each movie. In some cases, it might be difficult to tell what a movie is about from the small snippet. With an opening title, the opening title will be included in the small animations on the Scenes screen.

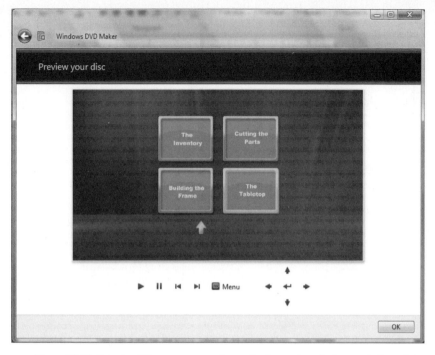

Figure 10-11. Opening titles on your movies make it easy to select a movie to watch.

Along the bottom of the preview screen, you'll see buttons that match most DVD player remote controls. Figure 10-12 explains their functions.

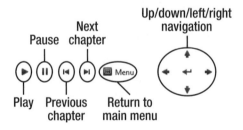

Figure 10-12. DVD remove control buttons are found on the preview screen.

Click the *OK* button to close the Preview screen when you're done, and return to the "Ready to burn disc" window (see Figure 10-9).

Once you've selected the menu option that you wish to use for your DVD, you can further customize it by changing items on the menu screen.

Click the "*Menu text*" button along the top of the screen shown in Figure 10-9 and you'll see a screen like the one in Figure 10-13. You can alter the text displayed on the main menu. I've changed "Scenes" to "Select Movie" (in Figure 10-13) to make it more explanatory for my viewers. Make any changes and click the *Change Text* button to implement your modifications.

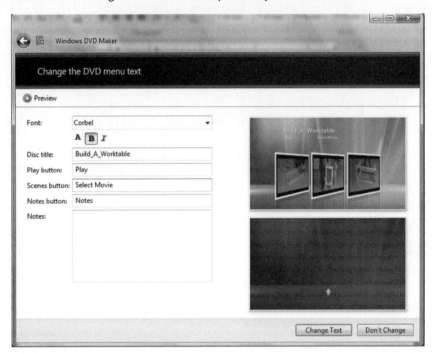

Figure 10-13. Change the title and other text items easily.

Next, I'll click the "*Customize menu*" button (see Figure 10-9), which opens the screen shown in Figure 10-14.

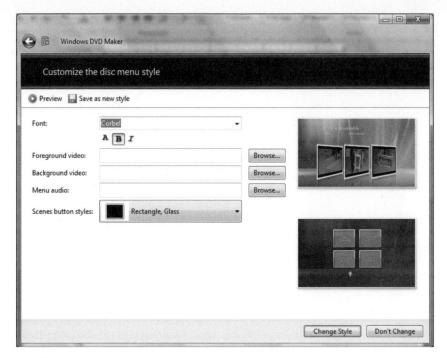

Figure 10-14. Additional menu options you can configure for your DVD.

I can change the font used for the DVD menu options by selecting a new one from the drop-down menu. I can also add background music to the main menu by clicking the Browse button next to "Menu audio" and selecting a song from my hard drive.

If I don't like the movie snippets (of the first video on the DVD disc) shown on the main menu, I can click the Foreground video and select one of the other movies I added to the disc. Likewise, the colorful backsplash provided on the menu can be changed to a movie (or even a photograph). A movie can be distracting at times, so be sure to click the *Preview* button to look at it and make sure it won't annoy your viewers.

Finally, you can change the scene button styles shown in Figure 10-14 by selecting a different button style from the "*Scenes button styles*" drop-down menu. Figure 10-15 shows the new buttons I've selected.

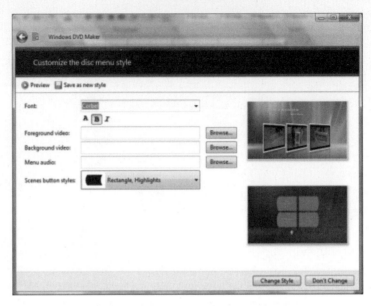

Figure 10-15. New button styles are easy to select and change.

After selecting my menu option and customizing it, I'm happy with the final design, shown in Figure 10-16. Now it's time to burn the disc.

Figure 10-16. My menu is completed, and I'm ready to burn my DVD.

Burn the Disc

I'm ready to create my DVD, so I'll click the *Burn* button shown in Figure 10-16. A window appears (see Figure 10-17) asking me to insert a blank DVD.

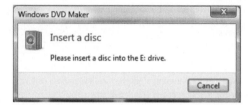

Figure 10-17. Inserting a blank disc gets the burn process started.

After I insert the blank DVD, a progress window appears, like the one in Figure 10-18.

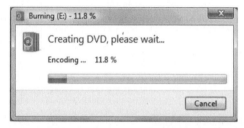

Figure 10-18. The DVD-burning progress bar.

I won't kid you, this could take a while. Movie Maker isn't exactly the fastest DVD burning software on the market, so take a break and come back and check the status every so often.

ExplainED

My four high-definition movies, totaling less than 20 minutes of video, took a total of 15 minutes to complete the DVD burn process. Your speed will depend on the DVD burner installed in your computer.

When the DVD burning process is completed, you'll see a window like the one shown in Figure 10-19. Your disc is ejected, and you can insert another blank disc if you want to burn another copy.

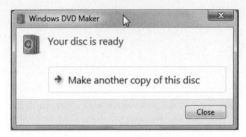

Figure 10-19. Congratulations! You've burned a DVD.

Click the *Close* button and you'll be returned to the "Ready to burn disc" window, shown back in Figure 10-9. Click the *Cancel* button to return to Movie Maker or make any changes you wish to the DVD main menu and burn another disc.

After clicking the *Cancel* button, you'll be asked if you wish to save your project. Click *Yes* and provide a name and location in the window that appears. This way, you can burn additional discs later (in case you lose the current one, for example) without having to go through movie selection and menu configuration.

Close Movie Maker and pop your new DVD disc into your computer or your DVD player ... it's time to watch some movies.

Watching the DVD

I've inserted my disc into my laptop. Figure 10-20 shows how Windows Media Player automatically opens to my disc's main menu.

I don't have a remote control, so I'll have to use my mouse to select movies to play and use the controls.

If I insert the disc into my DVD player at home, I'll be able to use my DVD player's remote control to select various options using the Up/Down/Left/Right buttons to navigate around the screen. I click the OK button on my remote to select a movie and the Play and Pause and Stop buttons work just like any other DVD I would watch.

Figure 10-20. Windows Media Player starts my disc's menu automatically.

The menu system definitely gives my DVD a polished look and feel, and viewers of my disc will be able to watch all four movies or select one of interest with the "Select Movie" option shown in Figure 10-20. With all my cropping, voice-overs, background music, opening titles, and more, my DVD will hopefully be entertaining to my viewers.

Of course, it doesn't stop there. Always ask your viewers about their experience with your DVD and see if there's any room for improvement. Some may tell you they don't like the background music or that you need to make your text larger (or a different color). If you saved your DVD project, it's a cinch to reopen it, make changes, and burn a new and improved DVD disc.

Have fun.

What's Next?

At this point, you should have a solid understanding of how to use Movie Maker to put together some great eye-catching and entertaining movies. Movie Maker is free, however, and sooner or later you're going to encounter a limitation. There are other video editing applications out there, but most of them are going to cost you some cash. Before reaching for your wallet or purse, however, I'd like to offer you some alternatives. Chapter 11 will cover a few video manipulation applications — some of them do only one or two things, but they do it well. In addition to these extra applications, I'm going to offer some tips and suggestions for improving your movies and making them the absolute best they can be.

Chapter 11

Tips & Advice

It seems that every time I edit a video clip or share a completed movie with my friends and family, I learn a new trick or discover a shortcut or specialty application that makes my final movies even better.

There is no shortage of movie-editing advice on the Internet, and a simple Google search will provide you with hours of reading and tips to try out for your next movie. It's a lot to sift through, so I'm hoping to give you a jump-start by providing you with some tips and advice that I've collected and applied to my movie editing over the years.

Some of what follows is simple suggestions that can help you the next time you're using your video recorder. Other information I'm providing includes links to Web sites where you can download specialty software for applying very specific or unusual actions to your movies.

The Internet contains more information on video editing and movie creation than I could ever hope to provide you in a single chapter. That said, I'll be providing you with additional Web sites to check out when you have time: sites full of advice for amateurs and professionals.

There is one piece of advice, however, that I wish to offer up right now: hunt down the manuals for your video recorder and digital camera, read through them, and get to know every feature offered by your devices. The more you know about how your devices work, the better your pictures and videos will look onscreen.

Advice from the Web

There are hundreds, maybe even thousands, of Web sites dedicated to photography and shooting video. The problem is wading through all the options. But with some patience, you'll find there's a lot of good stuff floating around out there for free on the Internet.

ExplainED

One suggestion I'd like to share here is to avoid professional videographer organizations' Web sites. Access to articles is typically limited or completely off-limits to non-members, and membership usually involves a fee.

Below are some great websites that I've found that offer articles specifically on videography.

- http://videoproductiontips.com/video-production-tips/videotaping-animals-tips-and-tricks/: Animals aren't always the easiest subject to video, so be sure to read this article, which contains some advice for working with our many-legged friends.

- www.babiestoday.com/articles/family-life/tips-for-videotaping-babies-6092/: Who doesn't love videos of babies and toddlers? Here's a great article on videotaping young children and babies.

- www.reelseo.com/holiday-video-tips/: We all shoot video during the holidays, right? Here's a list of eight great tips along with a video demonstrating techniques geared to shooting holiday movies.

- www.crutchfield.com/S-xz3lXFnUkAK/Learn/learningcenter/home/camcordertips.html: Twelve great tips for using your video camera and taking care of your videos.

- www.bealecorner.com/trv900/wedding.html: If you videotape weddings or wish to do so, don't ignore this great little collection of tips specifically for shooting and editing videos of weddings.

- http://chris.pirillo.com/50-youtube-and-online-video-tips-and-tricks/: Chris offers over 50 tips for video editing for YouTube and other online video services.

- http://multimedia.journalism.berkeley.edu/tutorials/shooting_tips/: There's more advice for professionals than for beginners, but still some good stuff in there.

LinkED

One of my favorite blogs is Lifehacker.com. I visit the site every day. Anything related to making your life easier, better, and less complicated can be found here. It's no surprise to find dozens of articles related to taking better photos and videos. Search the blog using keywords, and you'll find enough reading material to keep you busy for days. One good article I recommend can be found at http://lifehacker.com/214043/8-ways-to-shoot-video-like-a-pro.

The Internet is also a great source of video tutorials focused on, no surprise, shooting video! Here are a few videos for you to check out, all found on YouTube:

- www.youtube.com/user/videomaker: A large collection of how-to videos.

- www.youtube.com/watch?v=UjSsIQooAJg: Very simple tips, but worth watching.

- www.youtube.com/watch?v=l373-7pbA6M: Tips on shooting better vacation videos.

- www.youtube.com/watch?v=7q9fPtu88po: Tips on shooting birthday videos.

- www.youtube.com/watch?v=gnJyVdynZRQ: Outdoor video shooting tips, including lighting information.

LinkED

Check http://macdevcenter.com/pub/a/mac/2003/06/13/dv_tips.html for 10 great tips on shooting video. I hunted down and bought one of those light reflector discs for less than $10.00 from a photographer getting rid of his stuff on craigslist.com, and it works great!

Between the videos and web articles that focus on video camera usage, you'll find more information than you'll likely ever have time to absorb! But do spend some time reading the articles and watching some videos. We can all use some tips for making our videos better.

Specialty Software

For a 100 percent free application, Movie Maker contains some impressive features that allow everyone to make better movies. With the special effects, animations, transitions, and other features I've covered in this book, you've got everything you need to edit your videos and put together some outstanding movies to share with the world.

But Movie Maker doesn't have everything. Here are a few applications I've discovered that provide additional features that Movie Maker lacks.

Photos from Video

Although my video recorder can take photos, I rarely use this feature. And when you're videotaping an action scene, it's often not very easy to stop what you're doing to take a single photo. Fortunately, MovieSnapShot allows you to save a frame from any video as a JPEG image. See Figure 11-1.

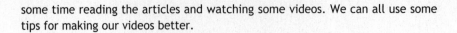

Download the free software at www.cd2html.de/moviesnapshot.en.html.

After downloading and installing the software, use the *Browse* button to locate and select a video. Use the *Play* and *Pause* buttons to locate the individual frame you wish to convert to a JPEG image. Finally, use the *Save* button to save the image and select the file's save location.

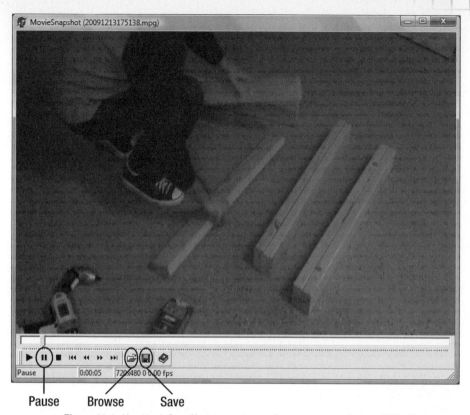

Pause   Browse   Save

Figure 11-1. Use MovieSnapShot to capture a frame and save it as a JPEG photo.

Create a Custom Opening Title

Movie Maker allows you to add opening titles to your movies, but the selection of fonts, font sizes, and colors is somewhat limited. One way to create a more fancy opening title screen is to use a slideshow application (like PowerPoint) to create the opening title, and then save it as an image to import into your Library.

LinkED

If you don't have PowerPoint (or a similar slideshow design application), download and install the free OpenOffice.org application at www.openoffice.org. It comes with a slideshow application called Impress that works similarly to PowerPoint.

Figure 11-2 shows an opening title screen I've created with PowerPoint 2007.

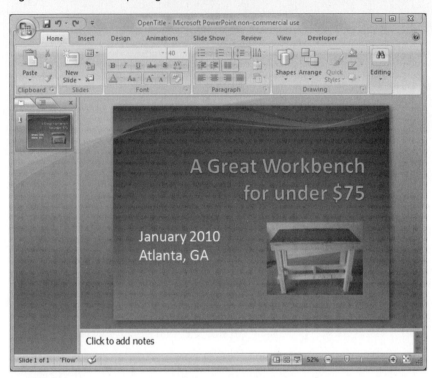

Figure 11-2. Use a slideshow application to design an eye-catching opening title.

After creating my image, I can save it by clicking the *File* menu, selecting *Save As*, and then clicking *Other Formats* from the fly-out menu. A new window will open that will allow me to select the location and file type. I'll save this image as a JPEG image that I can later import into my Movie Maker Library.

Figure 11-3 shows that I've added the image to my movie project and inserted it at the beginning of the movie. You can treat it just like a photo; change the duration time, add a transition or special effect, or even a voice-over.

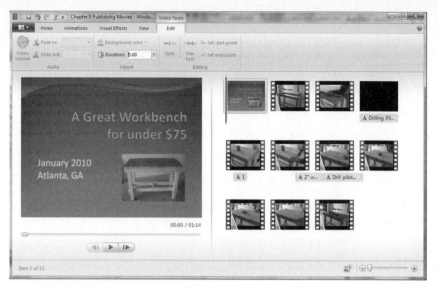

Figure 11-3. Add your custom opening title to your movie.

LinkED

If you've ever dreamed of including a Star Wars-style opening, with text scrolling by and drifting away into space, you'll be happy to know that someone has created a tutorial for using PowerPoint to mimic this feature. Find it at www.computorcompanion.com/LPMArticle.asp?ID=176.

You'll also need to convert this PowerPoint slideshow into a movie (to support the drifting text). Check out www.labnol.org/software/tutorials/convert-powerpoint-video-upload-youtube-ppt-dvd/2978/ for instructions on how to convert your slideshow to a movie.

Better Narration

Movie Maker allows you to import audio files and apply them to your movies, but it doesn't allow you to record your voice-overs or narration within the application itself. For that, you can use a Windows application called Recorder (covered in Chapter 4), but this little application doesn't really give you much in terms of editing power. You simply press the Record button, talk, and then save the file when you're done. Recorder keeps all the uh's an umm's and any tongue twisters you might have encountered during your narration.

And because Movie Maker will only allow you to add a single audio file to a video, you can't have both background music and a voice-over playing at the same time; not unless you record your narration while music plays in the background.

What's needed is a tool that will allow you to record your voice-overs and then go back and edit them just like you do with your videos: remove the bad stuff, keep the good stuff, and save it all in a file that can then be mixed with your background music.

Fortunately, there's a great (and free) application that can help you do all of this and more. It's called Audacity, and you can see it in Figure 11-4.

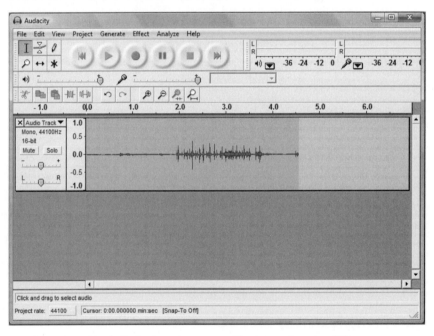

Figure 11-4. Use Audacity for voice-over and background music editing.

LinkED

You can download the free Audacity application by visiting http://audacity.sourceforge.net/.

Audacity is a power application: you'll need to spend some time reading over its documentation. Click the *Help* menu and select *Contents* to read over the built-in manual. Better yet, do a search on YouTube for Audacity and you'll find video tutorials showing you how to put Audacity to work.

What's Next?

Congratulations! You have mastered Movie Maker. You now have the knowledge to put all of its features to work making some great movies to share with the world. I have found that editing my movies with Movie Maker has made the process much more enjoyable. I don't have hundreds of special features and buttons and menus to figure out. I can get straight to work and spend less time putting together my final movie. I hope you've been able to see the simplicity of Movie Maker as well as the power of giving your movies a polished, professional look — videos that you'll be proud to share with friends, family, co-workers, and the rest of the world.

Now, go make some movies!

Index

You Need the Companion eBook

Your purchase of this book entitles you to buy the companion PDF-version eBook for only $10. Take the weightless companion with you anywhere.

We believe this Apress title will prove so indispensable that you'll want to carry it with you everywhere, which is why we are offering the companion eBook (in PDF format) for $10 to customers who purchase this book now. Convenient and fully searchable, the PDF version of any content-rich, page-heavy Apress book makes a valuable addition to your programming library. You can easily find and copy code—or perform examples by quickly toggling between instructions and the application. Even simultaneously tackling a donut, diet soda, and complex code becomes simplified with hands-free eBooks!

Once you purchase your book, getting the $10 companion eBook is simple:

❶ Visit **www.apress.com/promo/tendollars/**.

❷ Complete a basic registration form to receive a randomly generated question about this title.

❸ Answer the question correctly in 60 seconds, and you will receive a promotional code to redeem for the $10.00 eBook.

233 Spring Street, New York, NY 10013

Offer valid through 8/10.